Contents

TRIUMPH 1300 TC

TRIUMPH 1500

Introduction

This handbook has a specific purpose — to tell the owner or prospective owner of a Triumph 1300/1500 enough about the car so that it may be regularly and correctly serviced with the minimum of effort, thereby giving economical trouble-free transport.

It will also indicate what to do to get the car going again should it fail especially when a long way from home.

These models have been in production since 1965 (1500 since 1970) and are therefore available on the second hand market at reasonably low prices. As the purchase of a cheaper car is usually due to economic necessity it follows that garage servicing bills are equally to be avoided.

The reader will find in this handbook all routine maintenance tasks that are required to keep the car running well together with a list of the tools to do the job.

Most Triumph 1300 and 1500 models are now subject to the yearly MOT test; details of what the tester will be looking for, how to check these points, and the remedy of any faults are also given in this book.

Motorists reading this introduction will have had the unpleasant experiences at some time of having a car that for some reason or other simply 'dies' or just 'will not go'. Much of the work involved in looking after a car depends on accurate fault diagnosis in the first place. A comprehensive, methodical and progressive way of fault finding is therefore presented in this book. A great deal of time can be wasted in passing from one possible source of trouble to another. It is best and usually quicker to say at the start — 'This could be one of serveral things - let's get the book out'.

A considerable number of motorists worry about the state of their car, particularly when it has cost hundreds of pounds. We hope this handbook will help alleviate most of this worry by giving a prospective owner an idea of the condition of the car about to be purchased and what is required to keep it from causing worry during ownership.

After successfully using this handbook, should you wish to tackle the more complicated type of repair a most useful Owner's Workshop Manual is available on Triumph 1300 and 1500 models and is obtainable direct from the publishers or through all good accessory shops and booksellers.

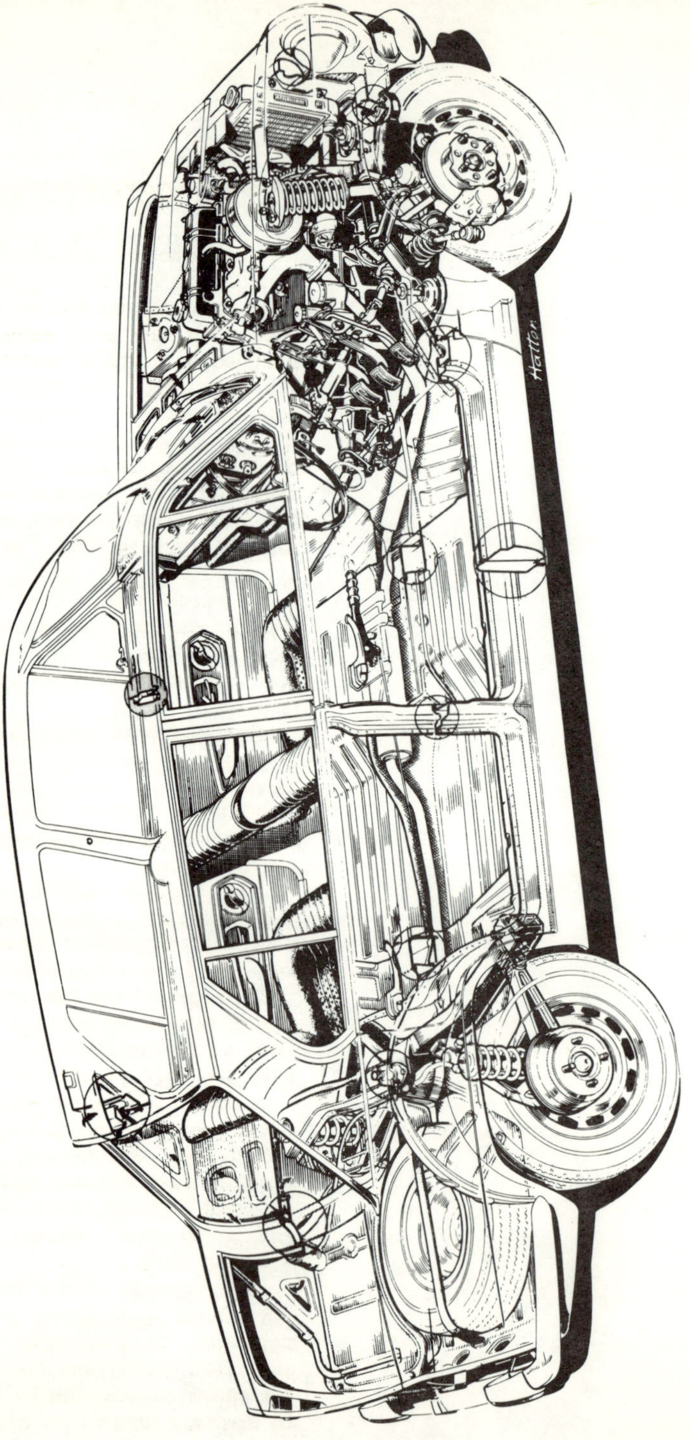
Hatton

Model identification

In October of 1965 the Triumph 1300 now heralded at its introduction as an advanced family saloon even though it did not actually appear for sale until early in 1966. It was designed as a smaller version of the 'de luxe' Triumph 2000 - or small car with 'big car' appointments. It featured front wheel drive with an integral engine, transmission and final drive, encased as a unit. The engine was basically that of the Triumph Spitfire, mounted in the conventional position, sitting on top of the gearbox and final drive. Two short drive shafts extended either side of the engine to drive the front wheels. Independent front and rear suspension was used, as were disc brakes on the front wheels and drums on the rear. It was a 4 door saloon, lavishly equipped inside, with a large boot.

Several special features were included which are normally only seen on larger, more expensive cars — adjustable steering column, ventilated upholstery, recessed window winders and door handles and a unique 'all in one dial' instrument panel.

The Triumph 1300TC appeared in October 1967 and was produced alongside the 1300. This was simply an increased performance version of the same saloon, distinguished by 'TC' badges on the rear and front side wings, having twin carburettors, a raised compression ratio, a modified crankshaft forging, a new camshaft and servo assisted braking system.

Upon the Triumph model range rationalisation within the BLMC group, the 1300 models were discontinued in late 1970 to be replaced by a similarly styled but mechanically different Triumph Toledo (not dealt with here) and a 'stretched' version of the 1300, the Triumph 1500.

The Triumph 1500 is still front wheel drive but with a larger stroke engine and a non-independent rear suspension using a 'dead' beam axle. Both bodily and mechanically similar to the earlier models, the 1500 is distinguishable by having a longer nose and a divided radiator grille with a '1500' badge in the centre and an extended boot.

Controls, instruments and indicators - 1300 model

1 Light selector switch
2 Roof light switch
3 Heater motor switch
4 Heater controls
5 Master lighting switch
6 Choke control
7 Speedometer
8 Warning indicator lamp cluster
9 Three-in-one instrument
10 Windscreen washer control
11 Windscreen wiper switch
12 Bonnet release control
13 Accelerator pedal
14 Brake pedal
15 Clutch pedal
16 Steering column control knob
17 Water valve control
18 Speedometer trip cancelling control
19 Direction indicator control
20 Ignition starter switch
21 Facia illumination rheostat
22 Horn bar
23 Handbrake lever
24 Gearshift lever

Control, instruments and indicators - 1500 models

1 Handbrake lever
2 Gear selector lever
3 Cigar-lighter
4 Variable direction heater oulet
5 Heater control panel
6 Instrument illumination rheostat
7 Speedometer
8 Warning light cluster
9 Instrument cluster
10 Fresh air vent
11 Choke control
12 Windscreen wiper and washer control
13 Heated back-light switch
14 Ignition starter switch and steering
15 Clutch pedal
16 Brake pedal
17 Accelerator pedal
18 Bonnet release control
19 Steering column adjustment clamp
20 Master lighting switch
21 Combination switch

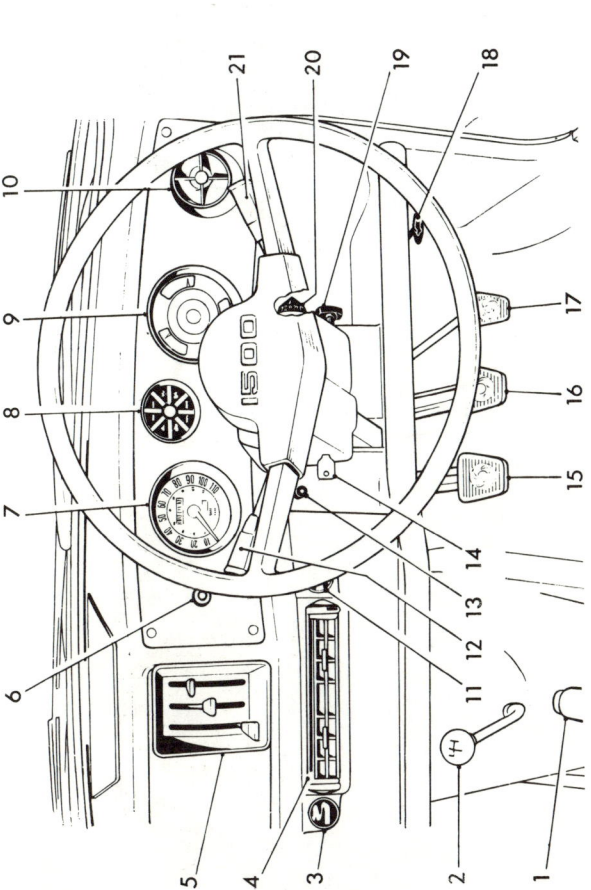

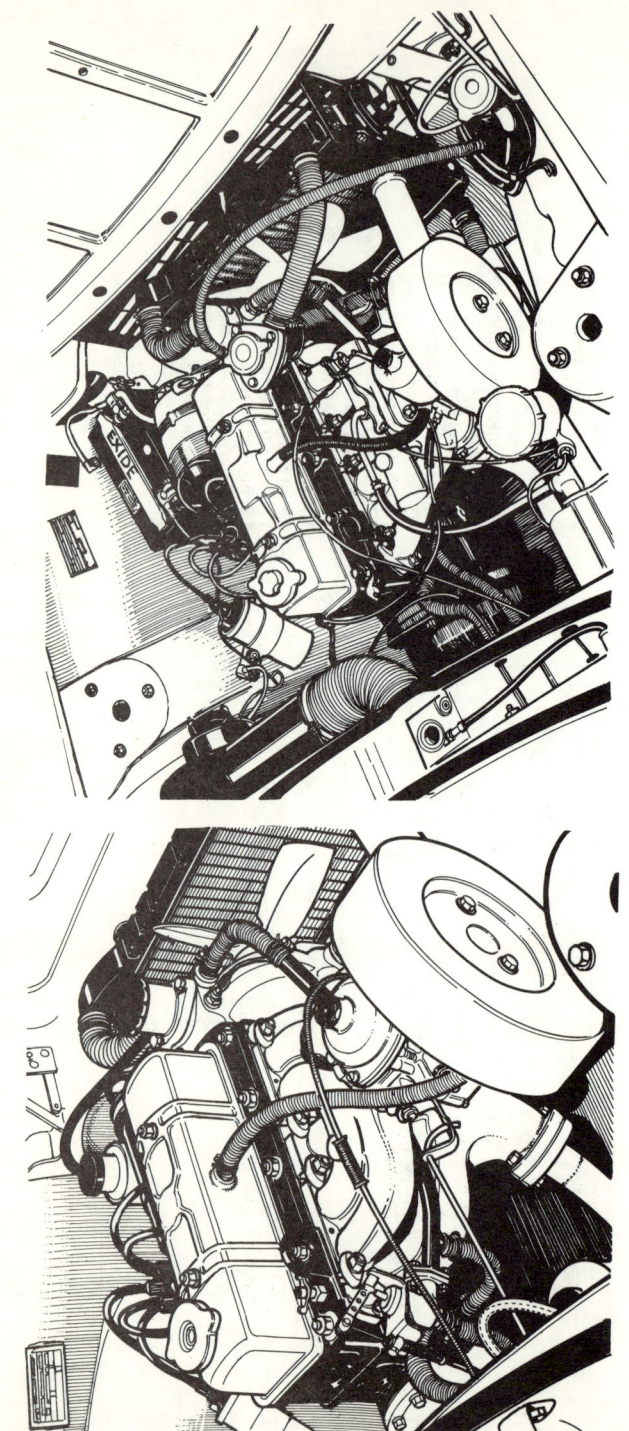

Under-bonnet views — (left) 1300 (right) 1500

Specifications, dimensions, weights, capacities

Engine
  Type   4 cylinder in line pushrod operated (ohv)

Type	4 cylinder in line pushrod operated (ohv)
Bore	73.7 mm (2.9 in)
Stroke:	
1300	76 mm (2.99 mm)
1500	87.5 mm (3.44 in)
Cubic capacity:	
1300	1246 cc (79.2 cu in)
1500	1493 cc (91 cu in)
Compression ratio:	
1300 and 1500	8.5 : 1
1300 TC	9 : 1
Maximum bhp:	
1300	61 at 5000 rpm
1300 TC	75 at 6000 rpm
1500	61 at 5000 rpm
Maximum torque:	
1300	72.91 lb ft (10.079 kg m) at 3000 rpm
1300 TC	75 lb ft (10.2 kg m) at 4000 rpm
1500	81 lb ft (11.198 kg m) at 2700 rpm
Firing order	1 3 4 2
Valve clearances (cold)	0.01 in (0.25 mm)
Sump capacity with filter	6.25 pints (3.5 litres)
Type of oil	Castrol GTX

Cooling system

Type	Pressurised radiator, thermo-syphon pump assisted and fan cooled
Coolant capacity (with heater)	
1300	6.25 pints (3.5 litres)
1500	8.5 pints (4.84 litres)
Blow off pressure of radiator cap:	
1300 prior to commission no.RD59522	7 lb/sq in (0.49 kg cm^2)
1300 and 1500 after commission no.RD59522	13 lb/sq in (0.91 kg cm^2)
Fan	4 blades, 12.5 in (31.65 cm) diameter

Fuel system

Tank capacity:	
1300	11.75 gallons (53.4 litres)
1500	12.5 gallons (57 litres)
Carburettors:	
1300 and 1500	Zenith Stromberg 150 CD
1300 TC	SU HS2 or HS4
Fuel pump	A.C. mechanical driven from camshaft

Ignition system
Distributor type — Lucas 25D4
Contact points gap — 0.005 in (0.381 mm)
Static ignition timing:
  Single carburettor — 9° BTDC
  Twin carburettor — 6° BTDC
Spark plugs — Champion N-9Y or AC Delco 45XLS (14 mm)
Plug gap — 0.025 in (0.64 mm)

Clutch
Type — Single dry plate diaphragm spring
Actuation — Hydraulic
Diameter:
  1300 — 6.5 in (165 mm) diameter
  1500 — 7.35 in (184 mm) diameter

Gearbox
Oil capacity
Gearbox oil

Ratios:	1300	1500
First	3.40	3.02
Second	2.16	1.918
Third	1.45	1.289
Top	1.06	0.889
Reverse	3.99	3.60

Final Drive
Location — Integral unit with gearbox and engine-hypoid level gears
Oil capacity — 1.25 pints (0.85 litre)
Final drive oil — Castrol Hypoy
Ratios:
  1300 — 4.11 : 1
  1500 — 4.55 : 1

Overall gear ratio
Overall gear ratios may be calculated by the use of the following formula:
Gear ratio X rear axle ratio = overall gear ratio

Steering
Type — Alford and Adler rack and pinion
Turning circle — 33 ft (10.06 m) approx.
Steering rack oil capacity — 0.25 pint (0.15 litre)
Steering rack oil — Castrol Hypoy

Suspension
Front — Independent, double wishbones and coil springs
Rear:
  1300 — Independent, semi-trailing arms, and coil springs
  1500 — Beam axle, non-independent, trailing links and coil springs
Shock absorbers — Telescopic, hydraulic

Wheels and Tyres

Wheels	Steel disc type, 4 stud fitting
Rim size	13 in (330 mm) 4S section
Type:	
1300	Dunlop C41
1500	Dunlop D75
Pressures:	
Front - 1300	22 lb/sq in (1.55 kg/sq cm)
- 1500	26 lb/sq in (1.83 kg/sq cm)
Rear - 1300	22 lb/sq in* (1.55 kg/sq cm)
- 1500	26 lb/sq in (1.83 kg/sq cm)

*Rear pressure to be increased by 4 lb/sq in (0.28 kg/sq cm) in the fully laden condition to provide optimum ride. NOTE: The recommended pressures should be taken when the tyre is cold, as a hot tyre normally shows a higher pressure.

Brakes

Type	Girling hydraulic, disc at front, drum at rear
Footbrake	Hydraulic on all four wheels
Handbrake	Mechanical to rear wheels only
Front brakes:	
Disc diameter	8.75 in (222 mm)
Rear brakes:	
Size:	
1300	8 x 1.25 in (203.2 x 3.175 mm)
1500	8 x 1.5 in (203.2 x 3.81 mm)
Disc brake details:	
Minimum pad lining thickness	0.125 in (3.18 mm)
Maximum disc run out	0.002 to 0.004 in (0.0508 to 0.1016 mm)
Disc pad material	Don 212
Front pad lining area	14.8 sq in (955 sq cm)
Front swept area:	
1300	145 sq in (9350 sq cm)
1500	165 sq in (10650 sq cm)
Drum brake details:	
Rear lining area	38 sq in (2450 sq cm)
Shoe lining material	Don 24
Minimum lining thickness	0.0625 in (1.588 mm)
Rear swept area:	
1300	63 sq in (4060 sq cm)
1500	75.5 sq in (4870 sq cm)
Adjustment:	
1300	Manually operated adjuster
1500	Self adjusting mechanism

Electrical system

Battery	12 volt lead acid
Earthed terminal	Negative (−)
Dynamo (1300)	Lucas C40−1
Alternator (1500)	Lucas 15 ACR
Control box (1300)	Lucas RB 340
Fuses	2 mounted on bulkhead

Bulbs

1300 models:

Headlamps (sealed beam)	60/45

Side parking	6
Front direction indicator	21
Rear direction indicator	21
Stop	6/21
Warning light cluster	1.5
Roof lamp	6
Number plate light	5
Instrument illumination	2.2

1500 models:

Front parking	5
Front flasher	21
Rear flasher	21
Tail/stop	5/21
Reverse	21
Number plate light	5
Luggage boot illumination	2.2
Roof lamp	6
Instrument illumination	2.2
Warning light cluster	1.5
Cigarette lighter illumination	2.2
Headlight - diameter	5.75 in (146.05 mm)

Dimensions:

Wheelbase	- 1300	8 ft 0.625 in (245.4 cm)
	- 1500	8 ft 0.625 in (245.4 cm)
Length	- 1300	12 ft 11 in (393.7 cm)
	- 1500	13 ft 6 in (411 cm)
Width	- 1300	5 ft 1.75 in (156.8 cm)
	- 1500	5 ft 1.75 in (156.8 cm)
Height	- 1300	4 ft 6 in (132.7 cm)
	- 1500	4 ft 6 in (132.7 cm)
Ground clearance	- 1300	5.5 in (14 cm)
	- 1500	5.5 in (14 cm)

Weights:

	1300	1500
Dry	17 cwt (843 kg)	18 cwt (915 kg)
Kerb	18 cwt (914 kg)	19 cwt (965 kg)
Max. gross vehicle weight	23.25 cwt (118 kg)	26 cwt (1315 kg)

Master lighting switch
— 1500
A Horns
B Headlights main
   beam lever
C Headlights flashing
   lever
D Master switch
L and R - Direction
indicators

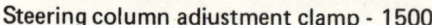

Steering column adjustment clamp - 1500

Road test data

	1300	1300TC	1500
Maximum speed (mph)	85	90	88
Cruising speed (mph)	70	80	75
Cruising range (miles)	330	315	330
Maximum speed in gears: 3rd	68	71	70
2nd	45	49	47
1st	29	31	30
Acceleration through gears (secs)			
0 - 30 mph	5.2	4.1	4.5
0 - 40 mph	8.3	6.9	7.2
0 - 50 mph	13.2	10.5	11.4
0 - 60 mph	19.0	15.9	16.6
0 - 70 mph	29.9	22.1	24.9
Standing start ¼ mile (secs)	21.8	19.8	20.5
Average fuel consumption (mpg)	28	27	27
Fuel consumption at steady 50 mph (mpg)	34	36	38

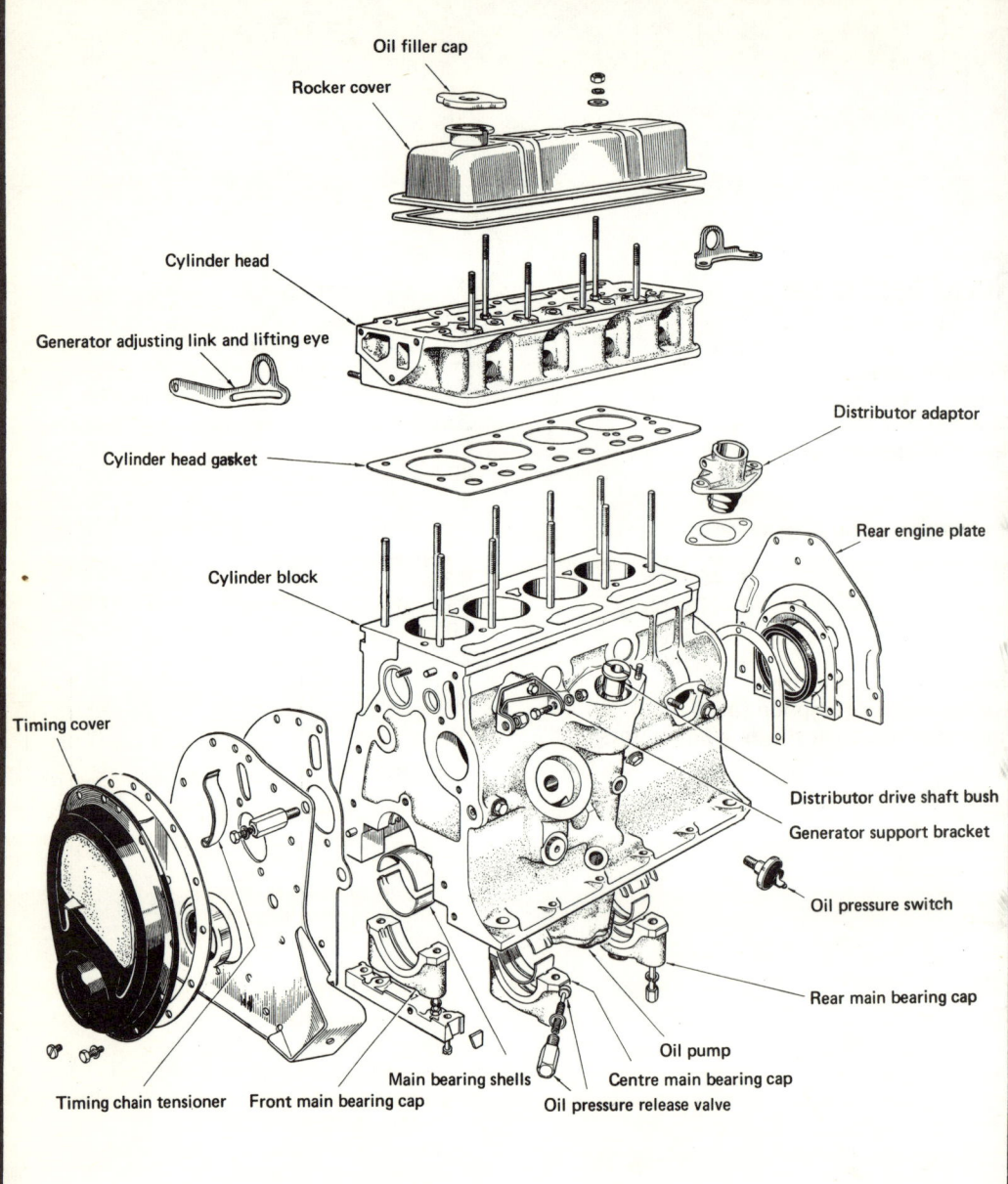

Oil filler cap

Rocker cover

Cylinder head

Generator adjusting link and lifting eye

Distributor adaptor

Cylinder head gasket

Rear engine plate

Cylinder block

Timing cover

Distributor drive shaft bush

Generator support bracket

Oil pressure switch

Rear main bearing cap

Oil pump

Timing chain tensioner   Front main bearing cap   Main bearing shells   Centre main bearing cap   Oil pressure release valve

Cylinder head and block fixed parts

Spares and touring pack

Before undertaking any long journey, whether in this country or abroad it is advisable to thoroughly check your car and its contents. It is better to have the car serviced in good time so that any maladjustments may be corrected. Breakdown services, accredited dealers and spare part availability for Triumph 1300 and 1500 models are not always there when they are needed particularly abroad and in outlying districts of Great Britain.

There are two lists, one giving spares which should always be carried in the car and the other suggesting those which it is advisable to carry if undertaking a journey abroad. Some dealers are able to supply manufacturers recommended touring packs on a hire/buy-if-you-use-basis.

Always Carry
First aid box and manual
Spare set of keys
Gallon can of petrol with filler spout (full)
List of Triumph main agents
Breakdown triangle (compulsory on the continent)
Torch (with red flashing dome)
Fan belt
Finilec puncture sealer
Roll of PVC insulation tape
Temporary plastic windscreen
Length of electric cable (heavy duty lighting circuit)
Screwdriver (medium sized)
Electrical screwdriver
Pair of pliers
Adjustable spanner (parrot jaw)
Distributor - rotor arm
Distributor - condenser
Distributor - set of points
1 tin of hand cleanser (Swarfega)

Going abroad
The articles in the 'Always carry' list
Tow rope
Set of light bulbs
Set of spark plugs - clean and correctly gapped
Inner tube and set of valves
Set of radiator hoses
Radiator sealer (Holts Radweld)
Set of fuses
Length of HT lead
Fire extinguisher
Tube of gasket jointing cement
Tin of Castrol Girling Brake Fluid
1 quart tin of Catrol GTX
1 spare head gasket set
Selection of tools
Adequate set of maps
List of Triumph agents abroad.

Always keep this handbook in the car and produce it if you break down abroad. Non-English speaking mechanics will find valuable information about your 'strange' car in it. There are many mechanical terms common to differing languages — you can always point at the photographs, it may help!

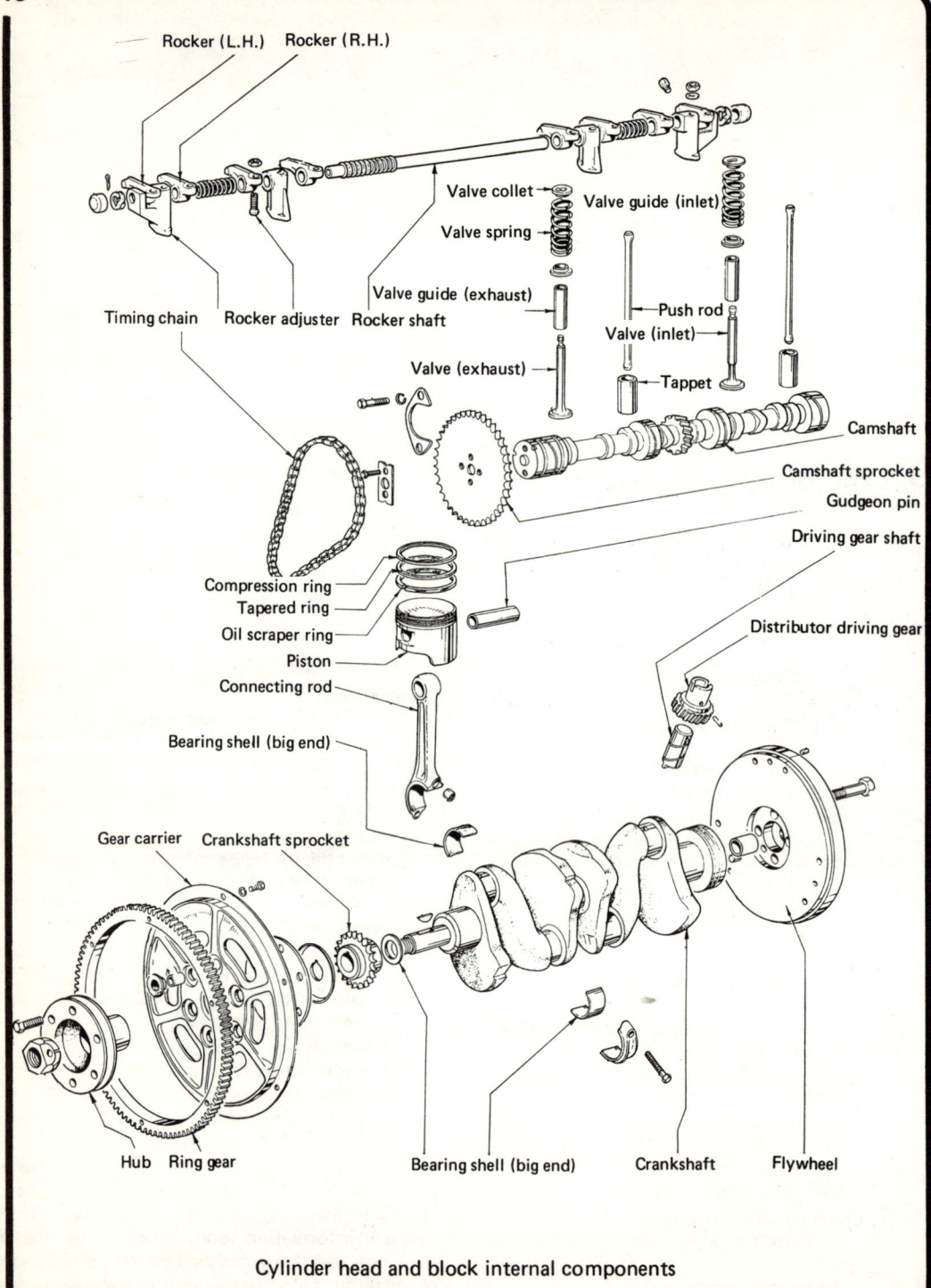

Cylinder head and block internal components

Tools

Routine Maintenance work requires a variety of tools to carry out successfully. Most motorists have pliers and screwdrivers, but certain other tools will need to be acquired for special tasks. Buy good tools. Cheap ones do not last and can be dangerous. Sufficient tools are listed below to cover the maintenance tasks described.

Open ended spanners, sizes:
- 5/16 AF
- 3/8AF
- 7/16AF
- 1/2AF
- 9/16AF

1 Adjustable spanner - parrot jaw 10 inch
1 Spark plug spanner
1 Pair pliers
1 Screwdriver - medium 8 inch
1 Screwdriver - crosshead 8 inch
1 Set feeler gauges
1 Brake adjusting spanner
1 Fine file - small
1 Engineer's hammer (1lb ball pein)
1 Soft headed hammer
1 Oil can (Castrol Everyman)
1 Grease gun (Castrol LM Grease)
Clean, non fluffy cloth
Overalls
Hand cleanser (Swarfega)

Service table

Service Interval	Necessary Maintenance Tasks Numbers relate to tasks detailed in the pages following
Daily	Carry out a quick check on lights, brakes, steering and tyres
Weekly or 250 miles/400 Km	1, 2, 3, 4, 5
Monthly or 1000 miles/1600 Km	6
Autumn each year	Renovate the bodywork and interior as detailed in Bodywork, Maintenance, Cleaning and Minor Repairs Chapter plus 38
6 months or 6000 miles/10000 Km	7, 8, 9, 10, 11, 12, 13, 14, 15, 16, 17, 18, 19, 20, 21, 22, 23, 24, 25
12 months or 12000 miles/20000 Km	26, 27, 28, 29, 30, 31, 32, 33, 34, 35, 36, 37
24 months or 24000 miles/40000 Km	39, 40, 41
36 months or 36000 miles/160000 Km	42

Routine maintenance

No matter how well you look after your car various components are going to wear out and need replacement but by carrying out the regular maintenance tasks listed below, you will be able to get above average mileage from your car before replacement becomes a necessity. A great many of the maintenance tasks are purely a visual examination of components, many are vital to the road-worthiness of the car and safety of its occupants. The whole business of routine maintenance may become a bit tedious at times but do not neglect anything; your life or some innocent party's life may depend on it and your car will appreciate the care you bestow on it by giving you virtually trouble free transport.

Plan ahead

Before starting work always read through what work is involved and make sure you have all the parts and lubricants that will be required. Most do-it-yourself motorists do their work during the evenings or weekends when the parts departments of garages are closed and nothing is more annoying than starting a job and being unable to complete it due to lack of spares.

Weekly or every 250 miles (400 Km)
1 Under the bonnet.

Check the oil level in the sump. The first reading taken on the dipstick should not be accepted as an accurate one. Wipe it clean and recheck. Top up if necessary with Castrol GTX.

Check the radiator coolant level in the translucent plastic reservoir and top up if necessary. If the level has dropped appreciably since the previous occasion check around for signs of a leak. If anti-freeze is in the coolant a leak will be more apparent as the coloured anti-freeze will be sprayed about by the fan.

Check the level of the electrolyte in the battery and top up with distilled water if this is

low. Do not overfill. If the battery is overfilled or any electrolyte spilled, immediately wipe away the excess as electrolyte, being a dilute solution of sulphuric acid, will attack and corrode any metal it comes into contact with. Check that the terminals are clean, secure, and coated with a petroleum jelly such as vaseline to prevent corrosion.

2 Steering.

Check the tyre pressures which are listed in the Specifications earlier in this book. Do not forget to check the spare.

Examine the tyres for unusual or excessive wear or damage. If an unusual wear pattern is developing take your car to your local garage to have the steering geometry and suspension checked.

Check that the steering is smooth and accurate. If the steering pulls one way or there is excessive play at the steering wheel take the car to your local garage for testing.

3 Brakes.

Check the level of the hydraulic fluid in the reservoir and top up with Castrol Girling Brake Fluid if necessary. If the level has dropped significantly examine the braking system for possible leaks.

4 Lights.

Check that all bulbs in the lights are in working order, including the flasher bulbs and brake lights.

If any of the bulbs are found to be defective they can be replaced in the following manner:

Headlight sealed beam unit.
1300 models: Remove the screw located at the bottom of the rim and with a wide blade screwdriver carefully prise away the rim from the wing. Undo and remove the three screws which hold the inner rim to the seating rim and lift away the inner rim.

Carefully draw the sealed beam unit

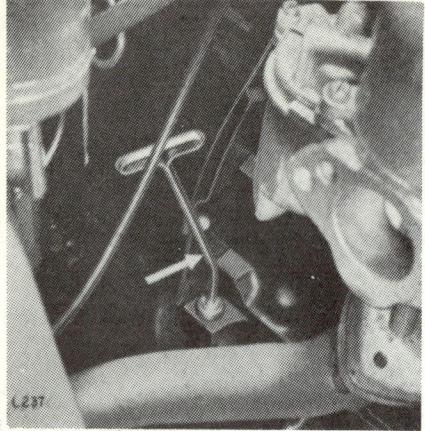

Engine oil dipstick

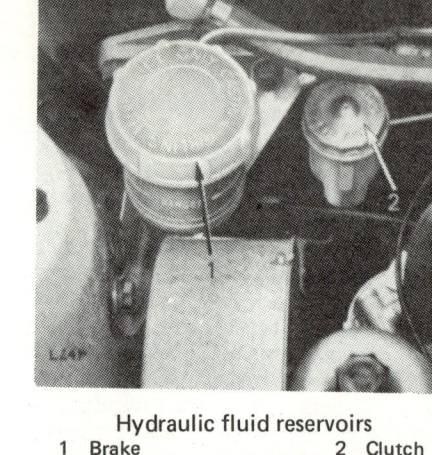

Hydraulic fluid reservoirs
1   Brake   2   Clutch

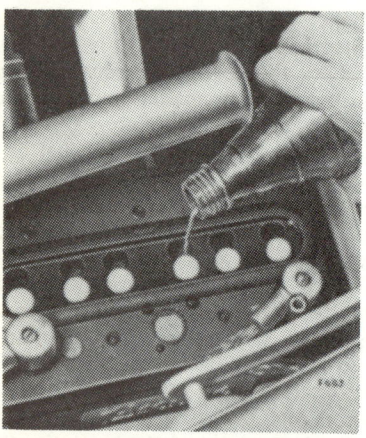

Topping up battery electrolyte

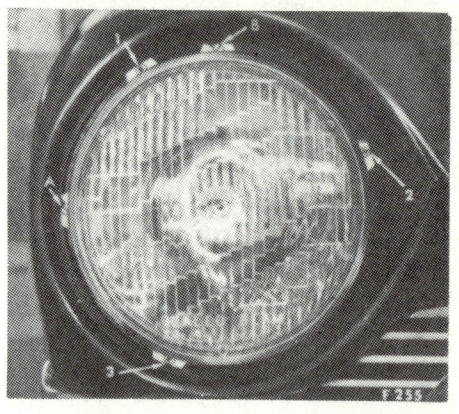

Headlamp sealed beam unit (1300)
1, 2, 3, Retaining screws.   A, B, Adjustment screws

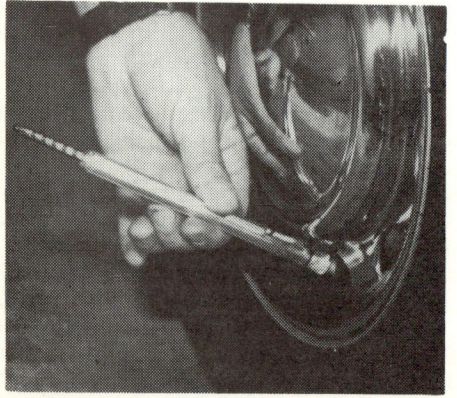

Tyre pressure check

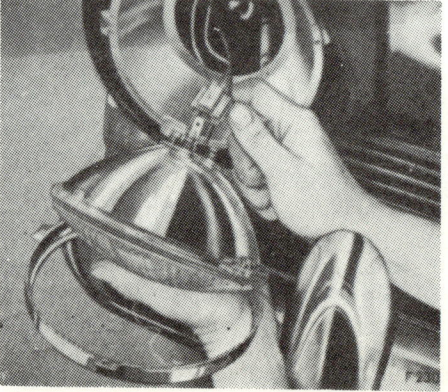

Disconnecting the sealed beam unit (1300)

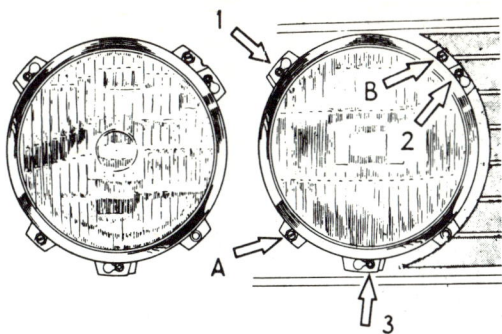

Headlamp beam unit (1500)

1, 2, 3, Retaining screws.   A, B, Adjustment screws

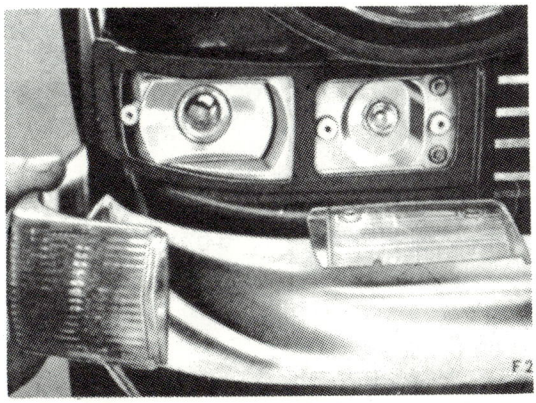

Side and front flasher lamps (1300)

Side and front flasher lamps (1500)

forwards until the connector is exposed and disconnect the sealed beam unit from the connector.

Replacement is a straightforward reversal of the above procedure.

1500 models: Undo and remove the two screws securing the bezel panel and lift away the bezel. Slacken the three screws securing the retaining rim and rotate in an anti-clockwise direction to release the retaining rim and light unit.

If a bulb is fitted, pull the connector from the bulb. Disengage the clip and withdraw the old bulb. Fit a new bulb making sure it is correctly located in the holder.

Where a sealed beam light unit is fitted, pull the connector from the light unit. Fit a new light unit.

Headlight alignment.

After replacing or disturbing a headlight unit it is advisable to have the headlamps aligned on proper optical equipment but if this is not available the following procedure should be used:

Position the car on level ground 10 feet (3.05metres) in front of a dark wall or board. The wall or board must be at right angles to the centre line of the car.

Bounce the car on its suspension to ensure correct settlement and then measure the height between the ground and the centre of the headlamps.

Draw a horizontal line across the board at this measured height and on this line mark off half the distance between the centres of the two headlights starting from the previously marked vertical line. This will give the centres of the headlights.

Remove the headlight rim (1300) or bezel (1500) and switch the headlamps onto full beam.

By carefully adjusting the horizontal and vertical adjusting screws on each lamp, align the centres of each beam onto the marks which were previously made on the horizontal line.

Bounce the car again and check that the beams return to the correct positions. At the same time check the operation of the dip switch.

Side and front flasher bulbs

1300 models: Unscrew and remove the three crosshead screws securing the two lenses. Lift away the lenses. The relevant bulb is removed from its holder by slightly depressing it and

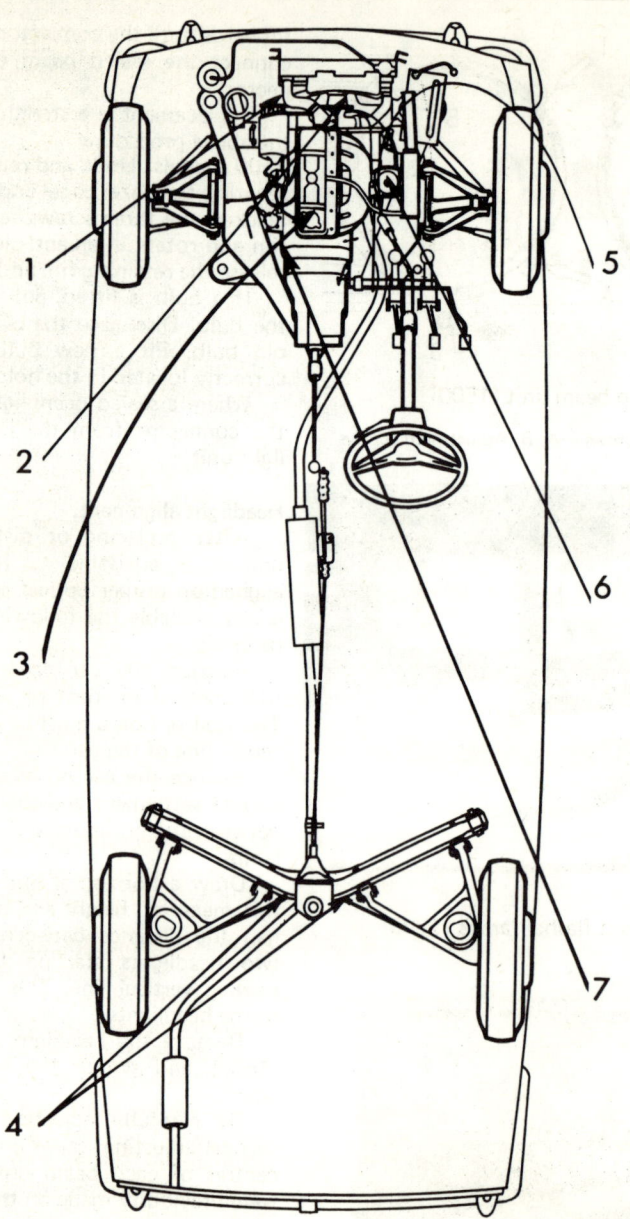

Lubrication chart

1   Final drive unit -
    Castrol Hypoy
2   Water pump - Cas-
    trol LM Grease
3   Engine - Castrol GTX

4   Handbrake cable
    guides and compen-
    sator - Castrol LM
    Grease

5   Steering box - Castrol
    LM Grease
6   Carburettor - Castrol

    GTX
7   Gearbox - Castrol
    Hypoy

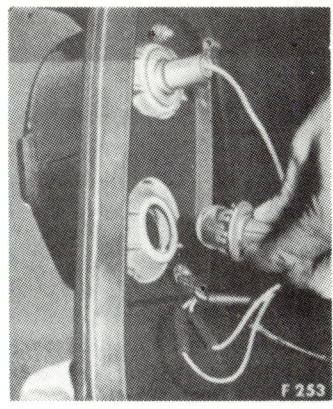

Rear flasher, tail/stop lamps (1300)

Rear flasher, tail/stop and reverse lamps (1500)

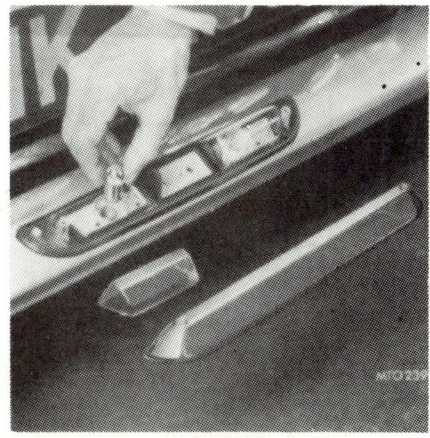

Number plate lamp

rotating it in an anti-clockwise direction. Re-fitting is the reverse procedure to removal.
1500 models: Undo and remove the two screws securing the complete light unit to the body. Draw the light unit forwards and remove the old bulb. Fit a new bulb and replace the light unit.

Rear flasher, tail/stop and reverse light bulbs
1300 models: Undo and remove the screws that secure the front edge of the boot interior trim. Carefully pull back the trim and remove the applicable bulb holder from the rear of the light unit. Fit a new bulb and replace the holder. Replace the interior trim and secure with the screws.
1500 models: Pull up the four fasteners and move the floor matting forwards. Undo and remove the five screws and turn back the rear trim the interior trim and floor matting. Note that a reversing light is also included in the rear light unit.

Rear Number plate lamp
    To renew the bulb undo and remove the two screws and lift off the chrome cover. Dis-engage the small lugs of the appropriate lens from the rubber base. Remove the bulb and fit a new one. Refit the lens and chrome cover.

5   Windscreen washer
    Top up the windscreen washer reservoir with clean water at weekly intervals.

Every month or 1000 miles (1600 Km)
6   Check master cylinder fluid
    Wipe the tops of the clutch and brake master cylinders, remove the caps and top up with Castrol Girling Brake Fluid. Take care not to spill any hydraulic fluid on the paintwork. Top up to the fluid level line on the side of the reservoir.
6,000 miles (10,000 Km)
    Every 6,000 miles or six monthly intervals if 6000 miles are not exceeded.

7   Engine oil change
    Run the engine until it has reached its normal working temperature. Place a container of at least 8 pints (4.55 litres) capacity under the sump drain plug, remove the plug and allow the oil to drain for at least ten minutes (Do not pour this old oil down a household drain. It is illegal. Take it to a local garage — they have special oil disposal facilities). Refit the sump.

Windscreen washer reservoir

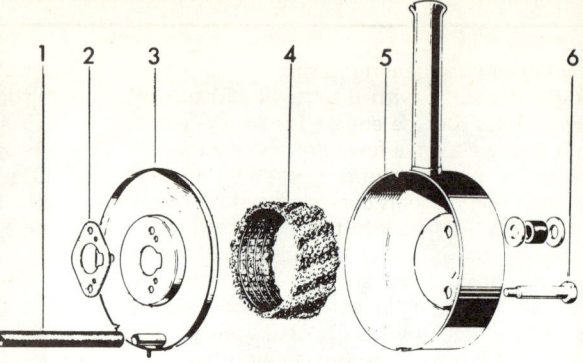

Oil wetted gauze type air cleaner (SC)

1	Rubber tube	4	Element
2	Gasket	5	Cover
3	Cover	6	Bolt

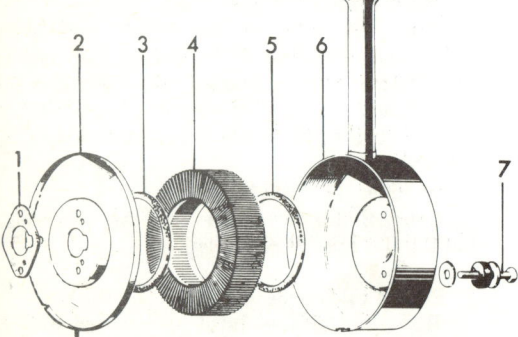

1 Sump drain plug   2 Gearbox oil level plug

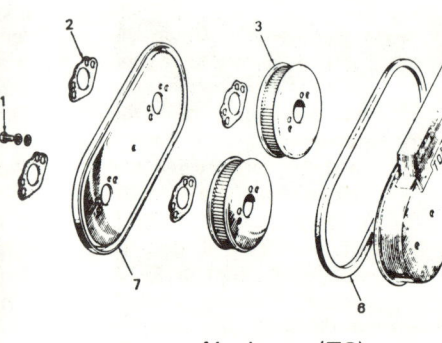

Air cleaner (TC)

1	Bolt	5	Body
2	Gasket	6	Seal
3	Element	7	Cover
4	Bolt		

Dry element air cleaner (SC)

1	Gasket	5	Gasket
2	Cover	6	Body
3	Gasket	7	Bolt
4	Element		

Topping up carburettor damper (SC)

drain plug and new sealing washer.

Refill the sump with 6 pints (3.41 litres) of Castrol GTX. Run the engine for a short while. Stop it and wait for a few minutes to allow the oil to drain into the sump. Check the dipstick to ensure the oil level is correct and if necessary top up to the high mark but do not overfill.

Remove the oil filler cap from the rocker cover and clean away any deposits from the gauze. Wash the cap in petrol and thoroughly dry it, dip it in Castrol GTX, shake the surplus oil away and replace it on the engine.

8 Air cleaner

On cars fitted with a single carburettor and a paper element air cleaner, detach the rubber tube (when fitted) and undo and remove the two bolts. Lift away the air cleaner. Take off the cover and lift away the element. Clean the element with a brush or low pressure air line. Every 12,000 miles (20,000 Km) renew the element. When refitting make sure that the gaskets are correctly located.

On cars fitted with a single carburettor and gauze element air cleaner, remove the element in the same manner as for the paper element. Clean the gauze element in petrol, allow it to drip dry and then dip it in Castrol GTX allowing for complete penetration of the oil. Surplus oil should be drained off and the element refitted. Make sure the gasket is fitted the correct way round.

The twin element air cleaner fitted to cars with twin carburettors is removed by first undoing and removing the four bolts securing the air cleaner to the carburettors. Lift the assembly clear of the petrol pipe. Remove the bolt and ease off the cover. Clean the elements with a brush or low pressure air line. Every 12,000 miles (20,000 Km) renew the elements. When refitting make sure that the gaskets are correctly located.

9 Carburettor dashpot

Wipe the top of the carburettor dashpot/s and unscrew the damper. Check the level of oil by using the damper as a dipstick. When the threaded plug is 0.25 in (6.35mm) above the dashpot, resistance should be felt. Top up with Castrol GTX.

10 Control lubrication

Lubricate all carburettor control pivots, linkage joints and cables with Castrol GTX. Also lubricate the accelerator pedal fulcrum.

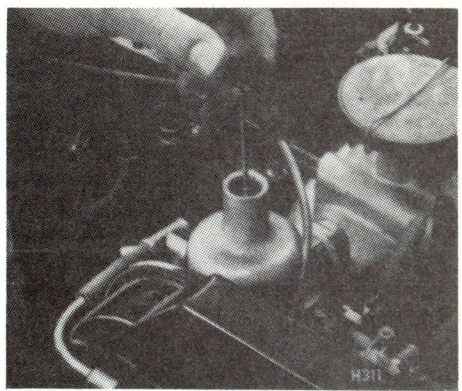

Topping up carburettor damper (TC)

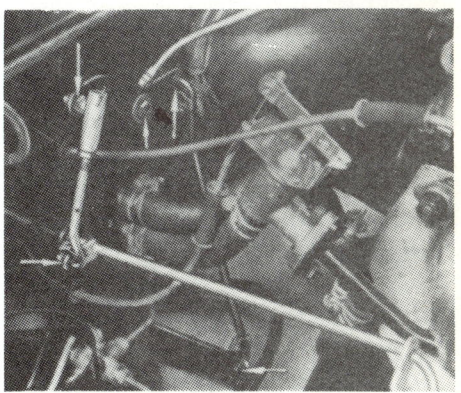

Lubricate the throttle control linkage at the points arrowed

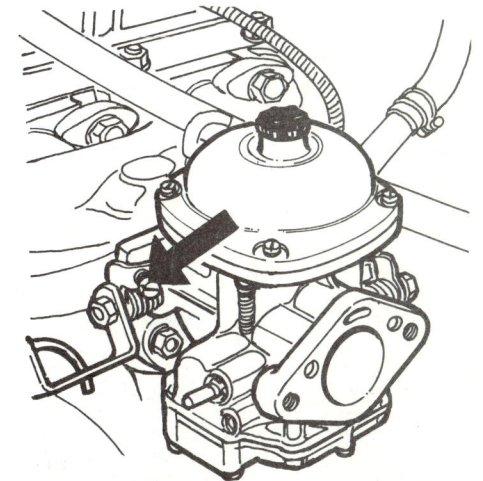

Stromberg 150 CD Carburettor - Throttle stop screw (arrowed)

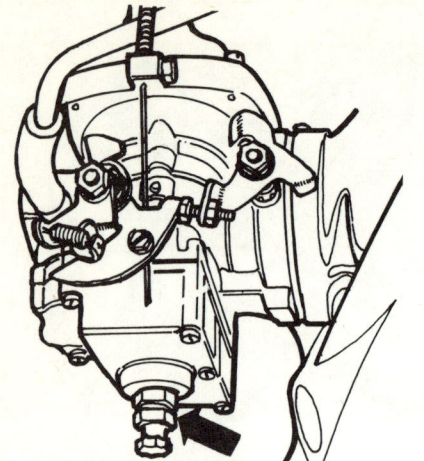

Stromberg 150 CD Carburettor - Jet adjusting
nut (arrowed)

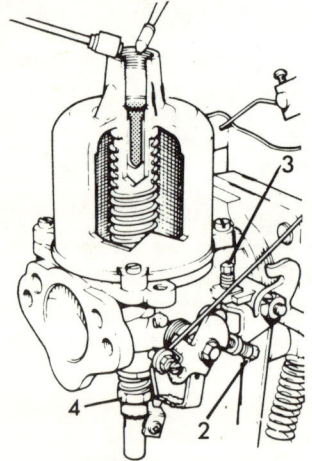

SU Carburettor
2 Fast idle screw
3 Throttle adjusting screw   4 Jet adjusting nut

Adjusting rocker arm/valve clearance

11 Engine idle speed
Stromberg 150 CD carburettor

To adjust this carburettor start the engine
and run until it reaches normal operating temperature. Remove the air cleaner, damper and
clip assembly. Press and hold the piston down
with a length of wire held in the oil well so the
underside of the piston rests on the bridge of
the choke. With a coin screw up clockwise the
slotted jet adjustment nut until the head of the
jet can be felt to just touch the underside of the
piston. Now turn the jet screw anti-clockwise
three full turns.

Start the engine and adjust the idle stop
screw so the engine runs fairly smoothly (about
600/650 rpm) without rocking on its
mountings. To get the engine to run smoothly
at this speed it may be necessary to turn the jet
adjustment nut a small amount in either
direction.

To check if the correct setting has been
found, lift the piston 0.031 in (0.794mm)
through the air intake with an electrical screwdriver. If the engine speed rises, the mixture is
too rich, and if it hesitates or stalls it is too
weak, Re-adjust the jet adjusting nut and recheck. Correct setting is obtained when the
engine speed does not increase when the piston
is raised by the required amount.

S U Carburettor

Set the engine to run at about 1000 rpm by
screwing in the throttle adjusting screw. Check
the mixture strength by raising the piston of
the carburettor 0.031 in (0.794mm) using the
piston lifting pin. If the engine speed increases
appreciably the mixture is too rich and con-
versely if the engine speed immediately
decreases the mixture is too weak. The mixture
is considered correct when the speed rises very
slightly.

To enrich the mixture rotate the adjustment nut which is at the bottom of
the underside of the carburettor, in an anti-
clockwise direction, i.e., downwards. Only turn
the adjusting nut a flat at a time and check
the mixture strength between each turn. It is
probable that there will be a slight increase or
decrease in engine speed after the mixture adjustment has been made, so that the throttle
idling adjustment screw should now be turned
so that the engine idles between 600 and 700
rpm.

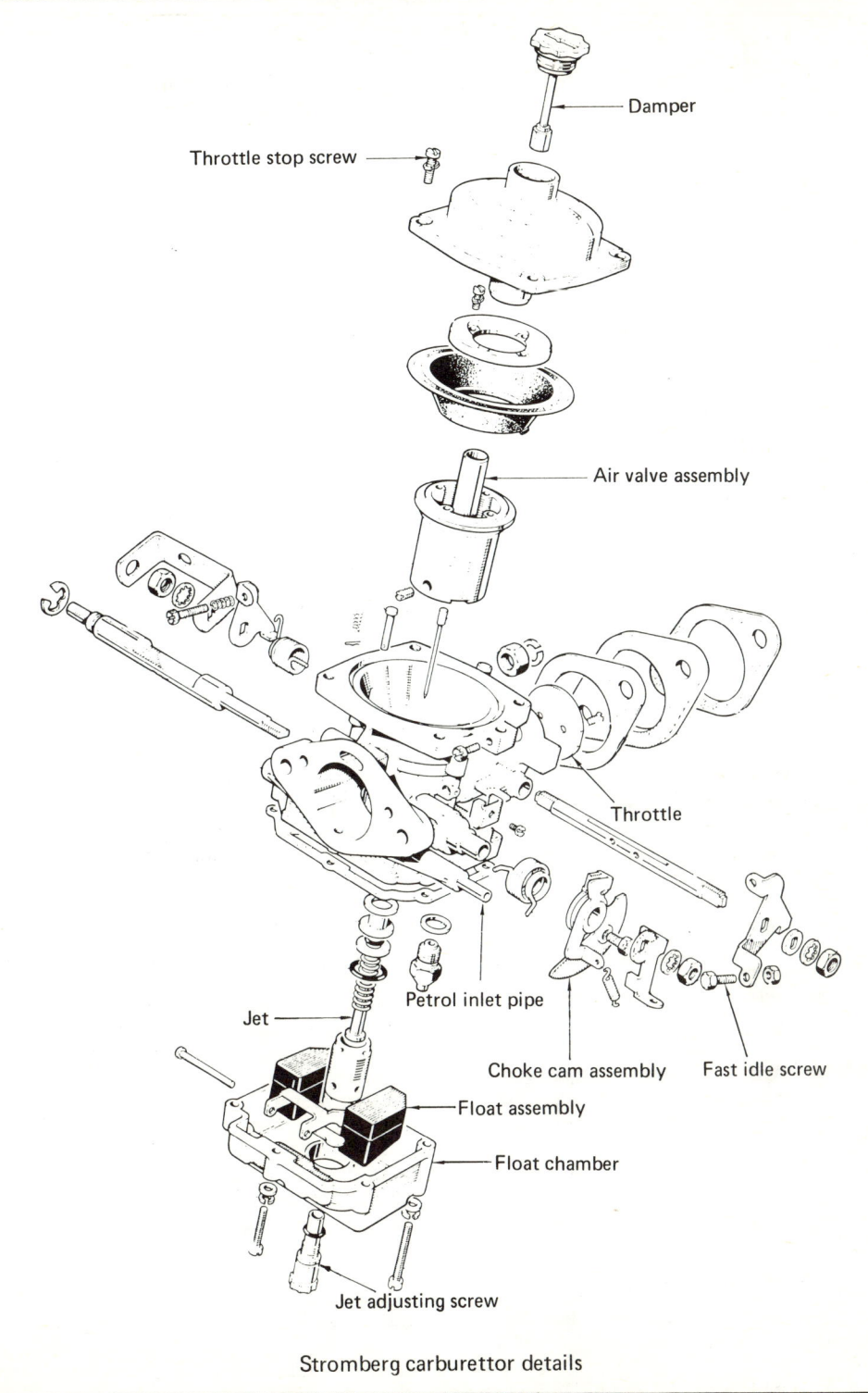

Damper

Throttle stop screw

Air valve assembly

Throttle

Petrol inlet pipe

Jet

Choke cam assembly

Fast idle screw

Float assembly

Float chamber

Jet adjusting screw

Stromberg carburettor details

12 Rocker arm/valve - adjustment

The valve adjustments should be made with the engine cold. The importance of correct rocker arm to valve stem clearances cannot be overstressed as they are vital to the performance of the engine. If the clearances are set to open, the efficiency of the engine is reduced because the valves open later and close earlier than was intended. If, on the other hand, the clearances are set too tight there is a danger that the stems will expand upon heating and not allow the valves to close properly, which will cause burning of the valve head and seat and possible warping.

Undo and remove the two holding down studs from the rocker cover, and then lift away the rocker cover and gasket.

Numbering from the front of the engine, valve numbers 1, 4, 5 and 8 are the exhaust valves and numbers 2, 3, 6 and 7 are inlet valves.

As it will be necessary to rotate the engine during adjustment of the valve clearances, remove the spark plugs to relieve the compression and find a socket or box spanner which fits the crankshaft pulley nut so it can be used to turn the engine.

It is important that the clearance is set when the tappet of the valve being adjusted, is on the heel of the cam (ie: opposite the peak). This can be done by carrying out the adjustments in the following order, which also avoids turning the crankshaft more than necessary.

Adjust valves	Valves fully open
1 and 3	8 and 6
5 and 2	4 and 7
8 and 6	1 and 3
4 and 7	5 and 2

The correct valve clearance of 0.010 in (0.25mm) is obtained by slackening the hexagonal locknut with a spanner while holding the ball pin against rotation with a screwdriver. Then, still pressing down with the screwdriver, insert a feeler gauge in the gap between the valve stem head and the rocker arm and adjust the ball pin until the feeler gauge will just move in and out without nipping. Still holding the ball pin in the correct position, tighten the locknut.

13 Spark plugs

Remove the spark plugs and clean off all carbon deposits. If your local garage has sand blasting equipment, this is the most effective method of cleaning plugs. Failing this a wire brush will suffice. Draw a fine file across the plug points to finally clear any remaining deposits, then check the gap between the electrodes. This must be checked with feeler gauges and should be 0.025 in (0.64mm). If the gap is incorrect the electrode attached to the plug body should be gently bent until the correct setting is obtained.

14 Hydraulic pipe inspection

Carefully examine all hydraulic pipes and unions for signs of leakage and flexible hoses for signs of perishing. Make sure that the front brake flexible hoses are not in contact with any body or mechanical component when the steering is turned on both full locks.

15 Tyre inspection

Check the tyre pressures with an accurate gauge and adjust as necessary. Make sure that the tyre walls and treads are free of damage. Remember that the tyre tread should have a minimum of 1 millimetre depth across three quarters of the total width of the tread.

16 Front and rear wheel alignment

The front and rear wheel alignment should be checked at the local Triumph garage (1300 models). On 1500 models it is only necessary to check the front wheel alignment.

17 Rear brake adjustment (1300 only)

Check the rear brake adjustment and adjust as necessary by screwing in the adjuster until solid resistance is felt. Slacken back one notch and this should allow the drum to rotate freely. If excessive binding is felt, slacken the adjuster a further notch. Binding should not be confused with normal drag caused by hub grease which will be particularly evident when cold.

18 Distributor

Pull off the two clips securing the distributor cap to the distributor body and lift away the cap. Clean it inside and out with a dry cloth. It is unlikely that the four segments will be badly burnt, but if they are, a new cap will have to be fitted.

Push in the carbon brush located in the top of the cap once or twice to make sure that it moves freely.

Gently prise the contact breaker points open to examine the condition of their faces. If they are rough, pitted or very dirty, it will be

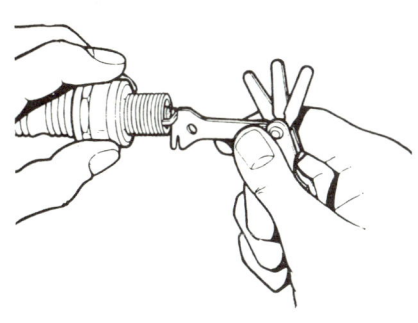

Check the spark plug gap

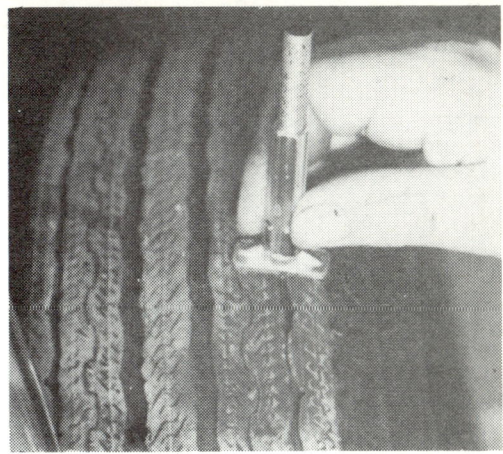

Check tyre tread depth

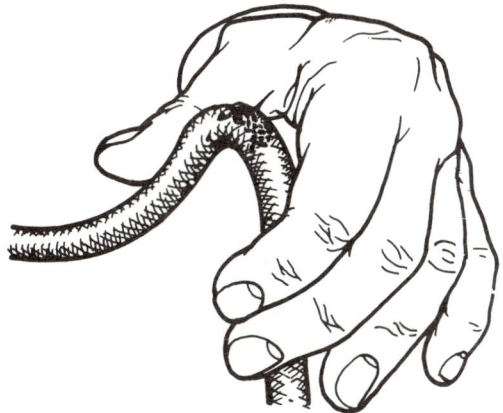

Examine flexible hoses for signs of perishing

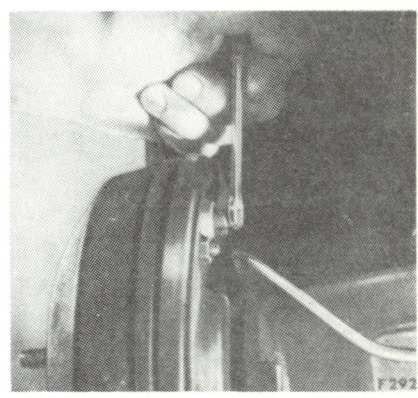

Rear brake adjuster (1300)

Distributor HT lead connections

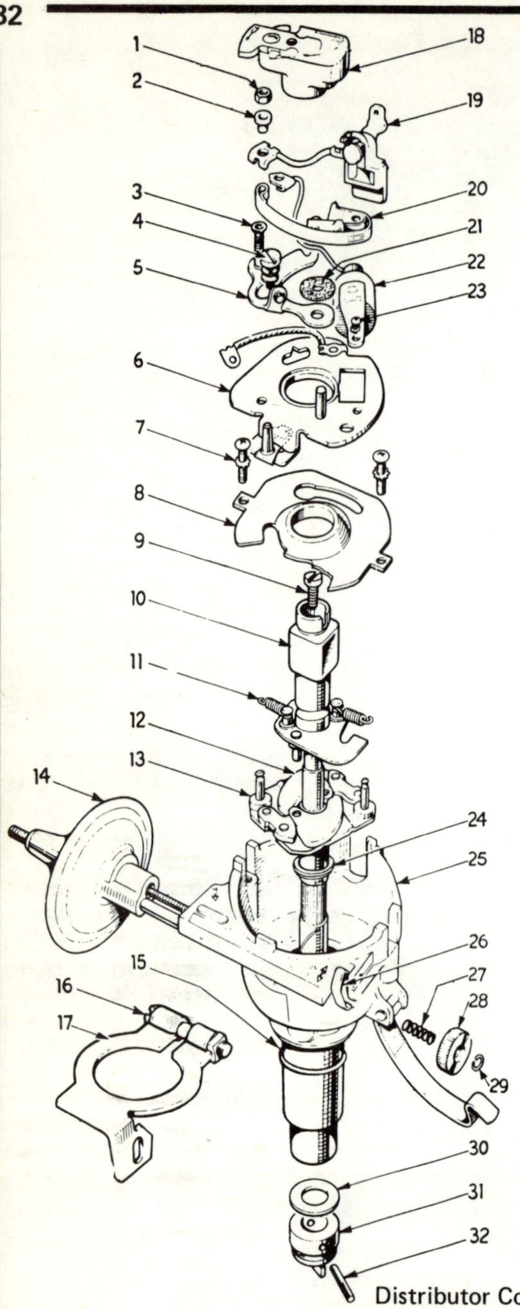

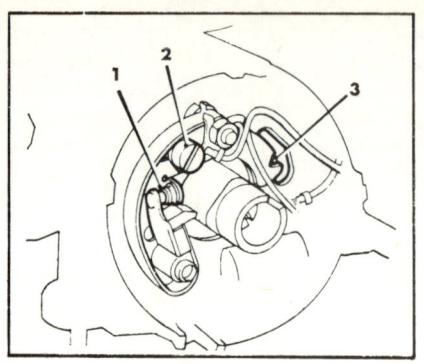

Contact breaker points checking

1 Gap
2 Contact assembly se-   curing screw
   3 Notched hole

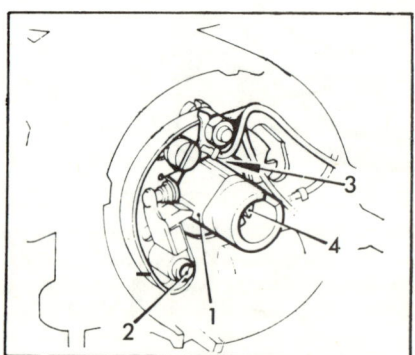

Distributor lubrication

1 Cam
2 Contact breaker pivot
3 Automatic timing mechanism
4 Centre screw

Distributor Component Parts

1	Nut	16	Clamp plate bolt
2	Insulating sleeve	17	Clamp plate
3	Insulating washer	18	Rotor arm
4	Fixed contact securing screw	19	L.T. terminal
5	Fixed contact	20	Spring contact
6	Contact plate	21	Insulating washer
7	Base plate securing screws	22	Capacitor
8	Base plate	23	Capacitor fixing screw
9	Cam securing screw	24	Thrust washer
10	Cam	25	Distributor body
11	Centrifugal spring	26	Ratchet spring
12	Centrifugal weights	27	Coil spring
13	Action plate and shaft assembly	28	Adjusting nut
14	Vacuum unit	29	Circlip
15	Oil seal	30	Washer
		31	Driving dog
		32	Securing pin

necessary to replace the contact breaker assembly.

Presuming the points are satisfactory measure the gap between the points by turning the engine over until the fibre (a nylon) heel on the contact set is on the peak of one of the four centre spindle cam lobes.

A 0.015in (0.381mm) feeler gauge should now just fit between the points. If the gap varies from this amount slacken off the screw which retains the contact breaker assembly, then insert a screwdriver in the oval notched hole at the end of the plate, turning clockwise to decrease, and anti-clockwise to increase the gap. Tighten the securing screw and check the gap again.

If it is necessary to fit new contact breaker points unscrew the terminal nut and remove it together with the washer under its head. Remove the flanged nylon bush and then the condenser lead and the low tension lead from the terminal pin. Lift off the contact breaker arm and then remove the large fibre washer from the terminal pin. The adjustable contact breaker plate is removed by unscrewing one holding down screw and removing it, complete with spring and flat washer.

Replacing a new set is a reversal of the removal procedure. Once the new assembly is in place adjust the points as described previously.

Pull off the rotor arm and apply two drops of Castrol GTX to the head of the large screw in the centre of the distributor. This lubricates the shaft bearings. Allow three drops of oil to flow past the base of the cam to the automatic timing mechanism. Smear a faint trace of oil on the cam itself. Apply a tiny spot of oil to the moving contact breaker pivot pin. Too much oil at this point will get onto the points and cause misfiring.

19 Gearbox oil level

With the car standing on level ground, clean the area around, and then remove the gearbox oil level plug. Top up the gearbox until the oil is level with the bottom of the filler plug threads, with Castrol Hypoy. This oil is sold in a special dispenser with a flexible tube which makes this job very easy.

Do not overfill the gearbox, and to ensure this has not happened, allow surplus oil to drain away for a minute or two before replacing the plug.

20 Final drive oil level

Wipe the area clean around the final drive oil level plug located on the front cover and remove the plug. Top up as necessary with Castrol Hypoy until the oil level is to the bottom of the plug threads. Allow surplus oil to drain away and refit the plug.

21 Steering rubber gaiters

Check the rubber gaiters on the constant velocity joints and steering assembly for leakage or damage. Check tightness of the clips where fitted.

22 Front disc brake friction pads - inspection, removal and replacement

Remove the front wheels and inspect the amount of friction material left on the friction pads. The pads must be renewed when the thickness of the material has worn down to 0.125 in (3.175mm).

With a pair of pliers pull out the two small wire clips that hold the main retaining pins in place.

Remove the main retaining pins which run through the caliper, the metal backing of the pads and the anti-squeal plate.

The friction pads and anti-squeal shims can now be removed from the caliper. If they prove difficult to move by hand, a pair of long nosed pliers can be used. Note the correct location of the anti-squeal shims as denoted by arrows for correct reassembly.

Carefully clean the recesses in the caliper in which the friction pads and anti-squeal shims lie, and the exposed faces of each piston from all traces of dirt and rust.

Remove the cap from the hydraulic fluid reservoir and place a large rag underneath the unit. Press the pistons in each half of the caliper right in − this will cause the fluid level in the reservoir to rise and possibly spill over the brim onto the protecting rag.

Fit the friction pads and shims and insert the main pad retaining pins and secure them with the small wire clips.

23 General lubrication

If the starter motor has been removed for servicing the Bendix drive should be lubricated with a little penetrating oil. Lubricate all locks, hinges, controls and striker plates. Wipe away any excess oil. Apply a few drops of glycerine to the wiper.

Final drive unit - universal joint coupling bolts
(arrowed)

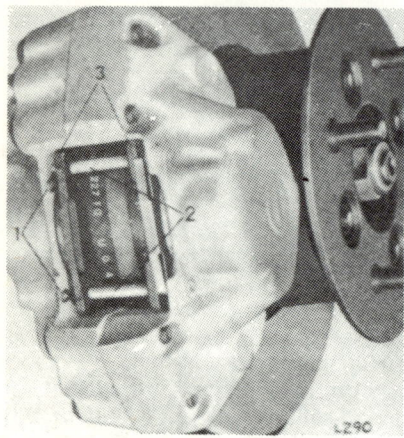

Front disc brake friction pads

1	Wire clips	3	Friction pads
2	Retaining pins		

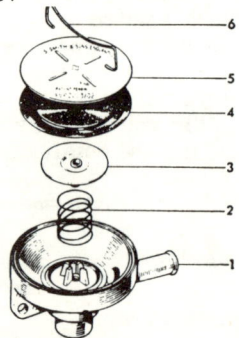

Crankcase breather valve

1	Body	4	Diaphragm
2	Spring	5	Cover
3	Valve pin	6	Clip

24 General inspection

Inspect the condition of all cooling system and heater hoses. Replace any suspect hoses. Check all fuel lines and union joints for leaks. Tighten the unions. Examine the exhaust system for leaks and holes and replace defective components as necessary.

25 Crankcase breather valve

To dismantle the valve, disengage the clip and lift out the cover, diaphragm, valve pin and spring. Clean all parts and inspect the diaphragm for damage. If evident obtain a new one. Reassembly is the reverse procedure to removal.

12,000 miles (20,000 Km)

Every 12,000 miles or yearly if 12,000 miles are not exceeded.

26 Water pump

Remove the water pump blanking plug and screw in a 1/8 Briggs taper grease nipple. Insert Castrol LM Grease until it issues from the pressure release hole in the side of the water pump.

27 Engine oil filter

Unscrew the oil filter canister from the side of the cylinder block and fit a new canister. To ensure an oil tight seal, wipe the joint faces and smear with a little Castrol GTX before screwing up the new filter tightly.

28 Fan belt - adjustment, replacement

The fan belt tension is correct when there is 0.5in lateral movement at the mid point position of the belt between the dynamo/alternator pulley and the water pump pulley.

To adjust the fan belt tension, slacken the dynamo/alternator securing bolts and move either in or out until the correct tension is obtained. It is easier if the securing bolts are only slackened so it still requires some force to move the unit. In this way the tension of the belt can be arrived at more quickly than by making frequent adjustments.

If difficulty is experienced in moving the dynamo away from the engine, a long spanner or screwdriver placed behind the dynamo and resting against the cylinder block, serves as a good lever and can be held in this position while the securing bolts are tightened down. Be most careful with the alternator casing.

If the fan belt is worn or has stretched unduly it should be replaced. The most usual

Location of water pump grease plug (arrowed)

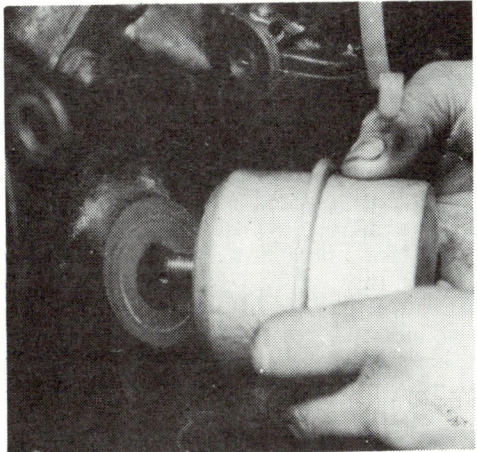

Fitting a new oil filter canister

Fan belt adjustment. 1, 2 Generator securing bolts

Fuel pump components

1	Retaining screw	13	Spring
2	Washer	14	Washer
3	Cover	15	Washer
4	Gasket	16	Retainer
5	Gauze	17	Spindle
6	Screw	18	Operating lever
7	Body	19	Return spring
8	Screws	20	Operating fork
9	Retainer	21	Distance washer
10	Valves	22	Priming lever assembly
11	Upper retainer	23	Lower body
12	Diaphragm assembly		

reason for replacement is that the belt has broken in service. It is therefore recommended that a spare belt is always carried.

To remove the belt, loosen the dynamo/alternator securing bolts and push the unit in towards the engine.

Slip the old belt over the crankshaft, dynamo/alternator and water pump pulley wheels and lift it off over the fan blades.

Put on a new belt in the same way and adjust it as just described. NOTE: after fitting a new belt it will require adjustment due to its initial stretch after about 250 miles (40 Km).

29 Drive shafts

Check the tightness of the universal joint coupling bolts, from underneath the car.

30 Fuel pump

Undo and remove the cover retaining bolt and fibre washer, lift off the dished cover, carefully remove the gasket and then lift away the filter screen together with the sediment which will have collected. With a tooth brush, clean the filter screen and inside of the pump upper body.

Inspect the cover gasket and if it is damaged obtain and fit a new gasket.

When replacing the cover, take care not to overtighten the centre screw, otherwise the thread inside the body of the pump will be stripped. If this does happen the pump will have to be removed from the engine, the hole drilled out and rethreaded for a larger diameter screw. The screw should only be tightened just enough to press the new gasket down to form an air-tight seal.

31 Dynamo

Inject a few drops of Castrol GTX through the hole in the rear of the dynamo to lubricate the rear bush. Check tightness of mounting bolts.

32 Handbrake linkage

Smear the handbrake compensator and cable guides with grease, take care to force it into the guide tubes and cable tracks.

33 Rear drum brake shoes - inspection, removal and replacement

At this mileage it is necessary to inspect the brake linings for wear. This will of course vary considerably according to how hard the car has

been driven. It is quite likely that only adjustment will be necessary and this is dealt with in Section 17.

Chock the front wheels, remove the rear wheel hub cap and loosen the wheel nuts. Jack up the rear of the car and place on firm supports to avoid any accidents. Remove the wheel nuts and lift away the road wheel.

Using a wide bladed screwdriver remove the two countersunk lead screws, holding the brake drum to the hub. Remove the brake drum. If the brake drum is tight slacken off the brake adjuster. If it will not move away from the hub, use a soft faced hammer and tap outwards on the circumference rotating the drum whilst completing this operation.

The brake linings should be renewed if they are so worn that the rivet heads are flush with the surface of the lining. If bonded linings are fitted they must be renewed when the lining material has worn down to 0.0625in (1.588mm) at its thinnest point.

Release the brake shoe web anti-rattle steady spring assembly by first rotating the locking retainer 90° and lifting off the washer, spring and second retainer. Slacken off the brake adjustment if not previously done.

Make a note that the lining on the leading brake shoe is fitted towards the trailing end. Observe the position of the brake shoe return springs, the interrupted spring being at the wheel cylinder end. Also note into which holes the springs locate in the brake shoe web.

To remove the brake shoe lift the trailing end of the shoe from the abutment in the adjuster tappet and the leading end from the wheel cylinder. Unhook the two springs from the shoe web and lift away. It is recommended that strong elastic bands are used to keep the piston in the wheel cylinder.

Thoroughly clean all traces of dust from the shoes, backplates and brake drums using a stiff brush. It is not recommended to use compressed air. Brake dust can cause judder and squeal and therefore it is important to clean out the brakes thoroughly.

Check that the piston is free in its cylinder, that the rubber dust covers are undamaged and in position, and that there are no hydraulic fluid leaks. Ensure that the handbrake lever assembly is free and also that the brake adjuster wedge is lubricated with a graphite based penetrating oil.

Prior to reassembly, smear a trace of Castrol PH Grease to all sliding surfaces and steady

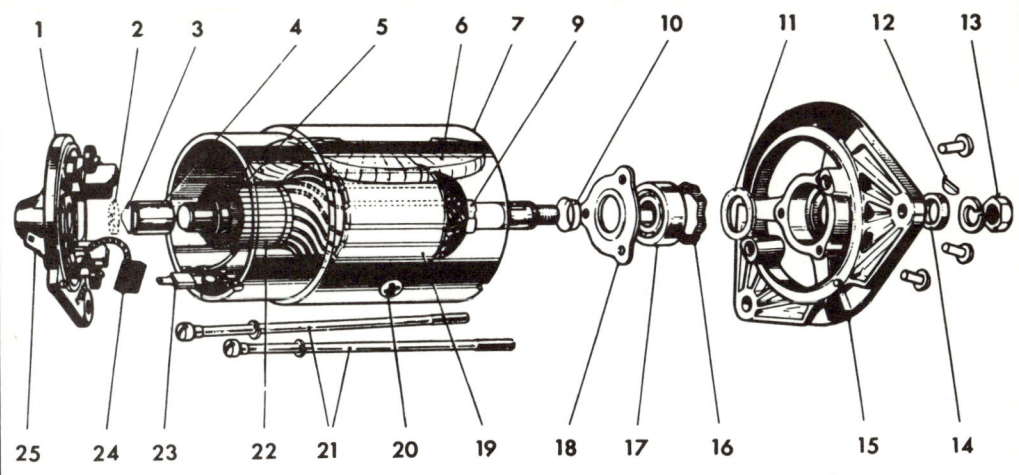

Component parts of dynamo

1 Commutator end bracket	7 Yoke	14 Pulley spacer	screw
2 Felt ring	9 Shaft collar	15 Drive end bracket	21 Through bolts
3 Felt ring retainer	10 Shaft collar retaining cup	16 Corrugated washer	22 Commutator
4 Porous bronze bush	11 Felt washer	17 Ball race	23 Field terminal
5 Fibre thrust washer	12 Key	18 Bearing retainer plate	24 Brush
6 Field coils	13 Pulley securing nut	19 Armature	25 Output terminal 'D'
		20 Pole shoe securing	

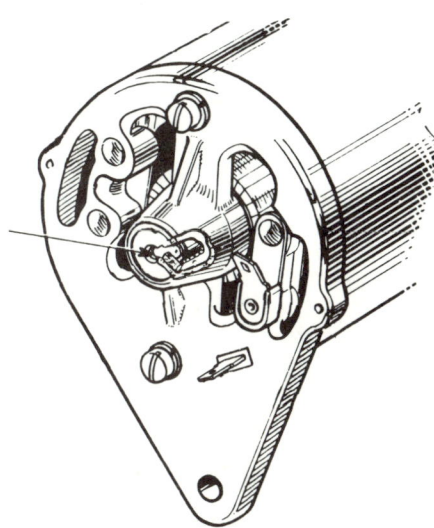

Dynamo rear bearing lubrication point

Lubricate handbrake compensator and cable guides

Rear drum brake components (top 1300) (bottom 1500)

posts. Do not allow any grease to come into contact with the linings or rubber parts. Refit the shoes in the reverse sequence to removal taking care that the two pull off springs are located in the correct web holes, correctly positioned between the web and backplate, and also the shoes register correctly into the slotted ends of the wheel cylinder and adjuster.

Back off the adjuster and replace the brake drum, retaining counter sunk screws and road wheel. Adjust the brakes as described in Section 17 (1300 models) or operate the handbrake until the ratchet 'clicks' four times before the brake is fully applied.

34 Steering

Apply a grease gun filled with Castrol LM Grease to the steering rack pinion housing. Do not give more than five strokes. Check the tightness of the steering unit attachments, tie rods and levers.

35 Servo unit (if fitted)

Unscrew the servo unit air filter cover retaining screw, lift away the screw, cover and element. Obtain and fit a new element and rubber washer.

36 Electrical - general

Inspect the ignition HT leads for cracking or deterioration and replace as necessary. Examine the dynamo brushes and replace them if worn. Fit new windscreen wiper blades.

37 Cooling system - anti-freeze

Every twelve months, probably in late September or early October, it is essential to add anti-freeze to the cooling system to prevent freezing of the coolant and possible damage to the engine in the coming winter months. Before adding the anti-freeze thoroughly check the complete system for signs of leaks and correct any if found.

It is also advised at this stage to flush the cooling system and thereby remove any rust scales or sludge which has accumulated over the past year. A description of how this is done can be found in the fault finding chart on Page 96.

To ensure complete protection against the coldest conditions likely to be encountered it is wise to have a 25% solution of Castrol Anti-freeze in the system. The coolant capacity with a heater fitted is 6.25 pints (3.5 litres) - 1300 models or 8.5 pints (4.84 litres) - 1500 models, you will need a 25% concentration to

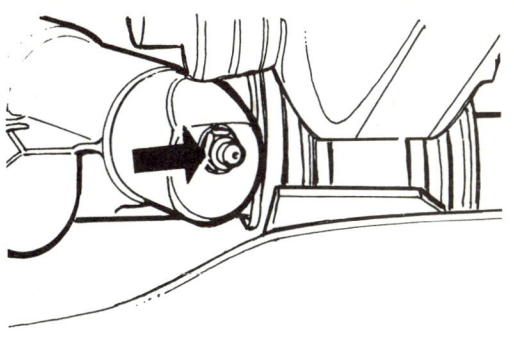

Steering unit grease nipple

Servo unit air filter

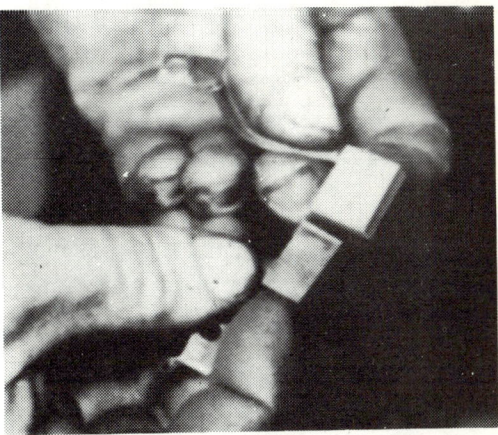

Old and new dynamo brushes compared

give protection to 10^oF (-12^oC) or 30% concentration to give protection to 3^oF (-16^oC).

Ideally anti-freeze and water should be mixed together in a separate container such as a watering can before the solution is poured into the radiator (having first closed the drain taps). If a container is not available pour in a little anti-freeze at a time followed by some water, thus ensuring a better mixing process. It may be found that not all the solution will go in at the first attempt and this is probably due to air-locks forming in the system. Should this happen, replace the radiator cap, start the engine, warm the car up and allow the coolant to circulate, thus removing the air-locks. Then top up with the remainder of the solution. Do not forget to put a little anti-freeze in the translucent reservoir.

38 Bodywork and underframe

Once a year or every 12,000 miles (20,000 Km), it is advisable to take your car to your local garage and have the underside of the bodywork steam cleaned. This will only take a couple of hours. This process will remove all traces of dirt and oil from the more inaccessible places and thorough inspection can then be carried out for signs of rust, frayed wiring, damaged hydraulic pipes, etc.

At the same time ask your garage to thoroughly steam clean the engine compartment. If steam cleaning is not available the engine can be cleaned with Gunk or a similar cleanser. Get hold of a stiff paintbrush and thoroughly cover the whole engine and engine compartment with the cleanser, working it well in where there is a heavy accumulation of oil and dirt. Be careful not to get any Gunk on the ignition system (coil, distributor, plug leads, HT lead, etc) but cover the system with oily water repellent rags. Finally, wash all the Gunk away with a hose pipe; as it is washed off it will take all the dirt and oil with it, leaving the engine looking clean and bright.

Get a can of Castrol Everyman lubricating oil, or if this is not available, ordinary Castrol GTX will do just as well, and apply a few drops of oil to the door, boot and bonnet hinges. It is also worthwhile giving a few drops of oil on all joints on the handbrake linkage and accelerator linkage to prevent sticky operation or seizure.

24,000 miles (40,000 Km)

Every 24,000 miles or 24 months if 24,000 miles are not exceeded.

39 Front hubs

Check the front hub bearing adjustment or wear by jacking up the front of the car and placing on firmly based stands. Grasp the top and bottom of the tyre and rock. If movement is evident the car should be taken to the local Triumph garage for further investigation.

40 Electrical

Check the tightness of the battery earth lead on the bodywork. Fit a new condenser to the distributor. Remove the starter motor, examine the brushes and replace as necessary. Clean the commutator and starter Bendix gear.

41 Braking system bleeding

Discuss with your local Triumph garage the advisability of renewing the brake hydraulic fluid. The old fluid should be drained out and refilled with fresh fluid. If bleeding the brakes

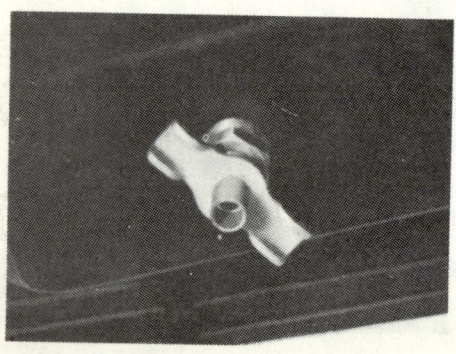

Radiator drain tap

Cylinder block drain tap

is to be done by the reader either as a mainten-ance job or because air has entered the system the following instructions should be followed. However, before actually starting carry out the checks listed below.

Examine the fluid reservoir cap to ensure that both vent holes, one on top and the second in the underside but not in line, are clear. Check the level of the fluid and top up if required.

Check all brake line unions and connections for possible seepage and at the same time check the condition of the rubber flexible hoses which may have perished.

If the condition of the wheel cylinders is in doubt, remove the brake drums as described in Section 33 and check for fluid leakage.

If there is any possibility of incorrect fluid having been put into the system, the complete system will have to be drained, flushed with methylated spirits and all rubber seals and cups removed. This is a lengthy process and is not within the scope of this book. Your local garage can do this job for you or if you wish to do it yourself the Haynes Triumph 1300/1500 Own-ers Workshop manual gives full details of the stripping and reassembly of all components.

Gather together a clean jam jar, a 9 inch length of tubing which fits tightly over the bleed nipples, and a tin of the correct brake fluid.

To bleed the system clean the areas around the bleed valves, and start on the front brakes first by removing the rubber cup over the bleed valve, if fitted, and fitting a rubber tube in posi-tion.

Place the end of the tube in a clean glass jar containing sufficient fluid to keep the end of the tube underneath during the operation.

Open the bleed valve with a spanner and quickly press down the brake pedal. After slowly releasing the pedal, pause for a moment to allow the fluid to recoup in the master cylinder and then depress again. This will force air from the system. Continue until no more air bubbles can be seen coming from the tube. At intervals make certain that the reservoir is kept topped up, otherwise air will enter at this point again.

Repeat this operation on the other front brake and the left hand rear brake, there being no bleed valve on the right hand rear brake. When completed, check the level of the fluid in the reservoir and then check the feel of the brake pedal, which should be firm and free from any 'spongy' action, which is normally associ-ated with air in the system.

36,000 miles (60,000 Km)
Every 36,000 miles or three years if 36,000 miles are not exceeded.
42 Braking system
Discuss with your local Triumph garage the advisability of renewing the brake cylinder seals, flexible pipes and changing the hydraulic fluid. This may not be necessary, but it is worth taking professional advice on this subject.

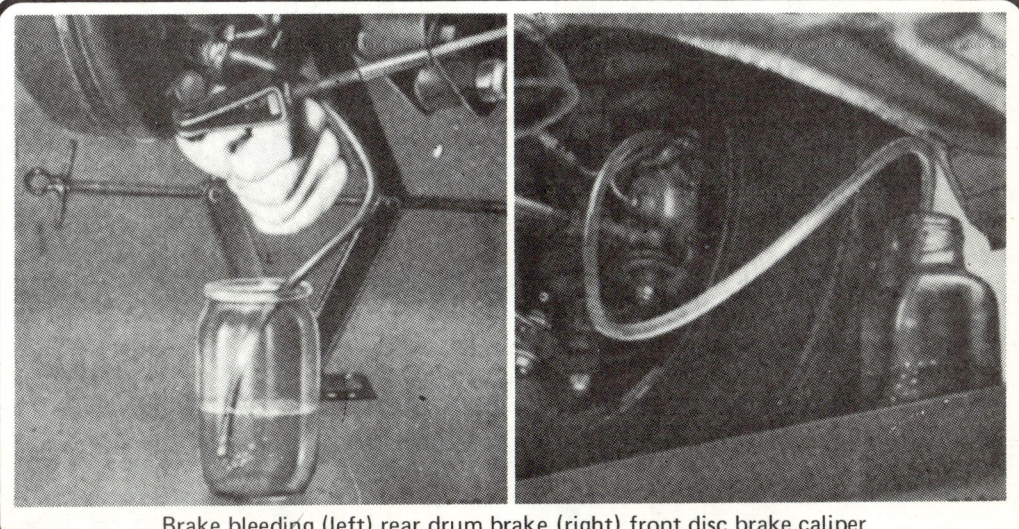

Brake bleeding (left) rear drum brake (right) front disc brake caliper

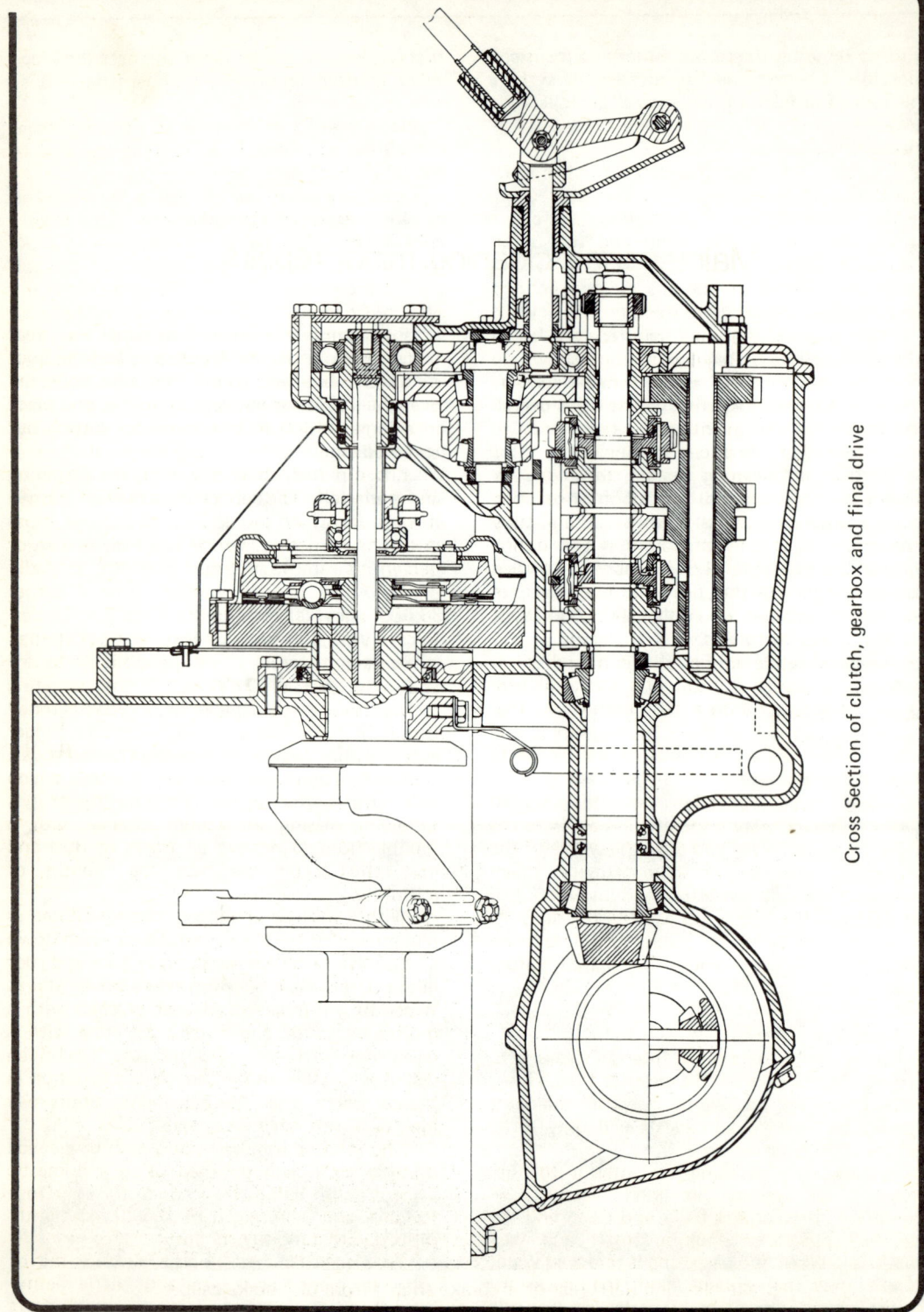

Cross Section of clutch, gearbox and final drive

Bodywork-Maintenance, cleaning, minor repairs

Introduction

Most owners like their cars to look clean and well polished. Regular cleaning shows up stone chips or rust marks which can be attended to before getting worse, the overall appearance is also maintained which tends to ensure a good re-sale price for the car.

Regular car cleaning can be considered by some as a necessary evil and only to be done when absolutely necessary whilst others enjoy this aspect of car care far more than the routine mechanical maintenance. The secret is to keep the car clean all the time so that it is not allowed to become too dirty making the work all that more difficult.

If you do not feel like doing the job all at one go then divide it into sections as done here in this Chapter, and do a little each week. This will give a continuous cleaning programme and enable you to do other jobs as well so as to break the monotony.

Should the car have been recently acquired and it is in a dirty state then take it along to the local Triumph garage and have the whole of the underside and engine compartment steam cleaned. This will save a tremendous amount of time. It is a very dirty job to do at home. Once clean it can be kept clean. See 'materials needed' section at the end of the chapter before starting.

Car cleaning - interior

Many car owners leave interior cleaning to last and prefer to wash the exterior first. This is really working backwards because the dust created by removal of carpets will only settle on the clean exterior.

By regularly cleaning the interior the upholstery will remain in good 'nearly new' condition, the carpets fresh and clean and the general appearance looking smart and well cared for. When the carpeting is removed water leaks may be evident and the necessary corrective action can be taken before rust sets in.

First empty the under dash panel tray, rear parcel shelf, under the front seats and the boot of all the bits and pieces that have collected over the last few months of motoring, and place in a large cardboard box ready for sorting out and replacing.

Lift out the rubber slip mats, the carpeting and underfelt. The rubber mats may be washed if very dirty, or just shaken to remove loose dirt. The carpeting may be brushed, shaken or beaten to remove the dust and dirt. If badly marked they can be washed using a carpet shampoo and laid out to dry in the sun. Underfelt should be carefully shaken but not washed or beaten otherwise it will be difficult to dry and may start to break up. If the carpeting around the pedals is worn it is recommended that it be renewed otherwise it can be a danger especially for lady drivers wearing heeled shoes.

Next lift out the rear seat cushion which will give better access for the operations following. Using a vacuum cleaner with a flexible hose to remove all traces of dust and grit that accumulate over the months of motoring.

With a suitable upholstery cleaner diluted as recommended by the manufacturer wash down all upholstery on the seats, body trim and roof lining. Use a neat solution on stubborn stains. Wipe off all traces of cleaner or soap with a moistened cloth and finally rub dry with a clean non-fluffy rag. Do not use too much water as it will cause excessive condensation in the car unless it is a hot day and the doors may have to be left open for a while.

The interior paintwork may next be cleaned using a cloth and polished using a domestic aerosol polish and a clean non-fluffy rag. Door handles and chrome trim should be lightly rubbed with a moistened cloth.

To clean the interior glass, interior mirror and instrument cluster glass add a little methylated spirits to water and wipe over with a soft cloth. Do not use ordinary domestic cleaners as they can cause smearing.

Inspect the seat belts for damage and make sure that the anchorages are still firm. The webbing may be washed in warm soapy water and wiped dry with an old towel.

Wash down the door, boot lid, and bonnet apertures and the edges of the doors, boot lid and bonnet. Remove all traces of lubricant with a paraffin moistened cloth. Take care to clean around the door hinges and locks as these are dust traps.

With a piece of wire probe the door drain holes to make sure that they are free of blockage. Inspect the floor pan for signs of rusting or leaking at the various seams. De-rust using Kurust and seal with a flexible sealing compound such as Seelastik.

Whilst the front doors are open make sure that the little courtesy light switches located in the door pillars operate freely. Check the bulb in the courtesy light for operation or for a disconnected cable at the rear of the switch if the bulb does not light.

Next go round all nuts, bolts and screws and make sure that all are tight and then lubricate the door locks and hinges, courtesy light switch plunger, choke control and front seat runners to ensure precise and free movement.

Turning to the boot, remove the complete contents including spare wheel and vacuum out all the accumulated dust and dirt. Wipe the paintwork down with a damp cloth. If carpeting is fitted clean this in a similar manner to the interior carpeting. Again look for water leaks especially in the corners and if necessary seal with Seelastik once the rust has been neutralised. Clear the drain holes using a piece of wire.

Using an oil can lubricate the handbrake lever assembly and the pedal pivots. Inspect the pedal rubbers for signs of excessive wear and fit new ones if necessary. It is dangerous to drive with worn pedal rubbers for on a wet day it is easy for the foot to accidentally slip off the pedal.

Should you have a slight tear on one of the seats or trim panel, cut a piece of spare trim from the underside of one of the seats and apply a coat of impact adhesive such as clear Bostik. Insert the patch into the hole with the glue uppermost and then apply adhesive to the flap of the trim section. Allow the recommended drying time to pass and then press down the torn edges, trying to get the edges as

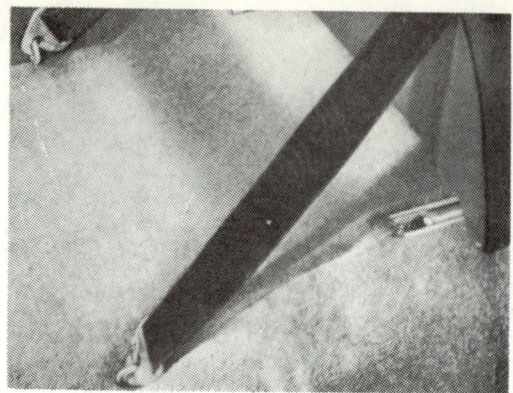

Front seat belt anchorage to the floor

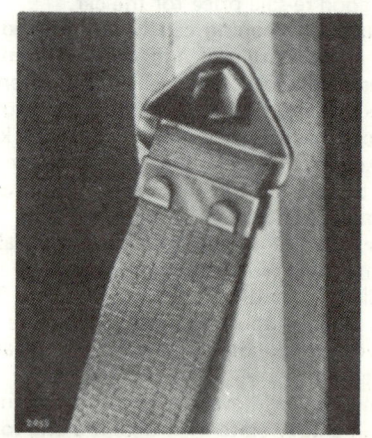

Front seat belt anchorage to the central door pillar

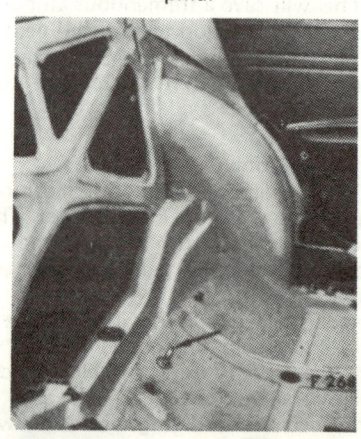

Rear seat belt lower anchorages

Wheel removing sequence

close together as possible which will make the repair less pronounced. Any large tears will have to be repaired using a piece of matching material which is obtainable from the local Triumph Distributor.

The time has now come for touching up the interior paintwork and full details for this will be found later in this Chapter. Once the paint is dry, the rear seat cushion and carpeting may be refitted followed by the articles that live on the parcel shelf and in the boot.

This is a good time to check the contents of the first aid kit, if carried, and any deficiencies should be made up. Check the tools in the car tool roll and lubricate the threads of the jack. Stow away the contents of the boot making sure that the main tool kit is so situated where it will not slide around or rattle.

Car cleaning - exterior (underside)

It was recommended in the introduction to this Chapter that if the car is in a dirty state it be taken to the local agents for steam cleaning.

With the underside relatively clean it is an easy matter to keep it clean. Remove the interior carpeting and contents of the boot. Jack up the car as high as possible and remove the road wheels. With a garden hose, a stiff brush, tin of paraffin and scraper and of course suitably clad for this work, soak the dirt accumulated under the wheel arches and crevices, loosening where necessary with the hand scraper. This will require time and patience but working systematically, front to rear, remove dirt and oil.

Whilst the underside of the car is drying check the seams for signs of leaking. Also generally check the tightness of all nuts and bolts and make sure the various pipes and wires are securely clipped to the underside of the body floor pan.

Inspect the underside for signs of rusting and, if evident, clear with a wire brush and neutralise with Kurust. When the underside is really dry, seal any leaking seams with a flexible sealing compound. Wipe off the Kurust with a rag soaked in methylated spirits and apply a coat of suitable red oxide cellulose primer surfacer. Allow to dry and if the part is visible finish off with a coat of Holts car enamel spray of the matching body paint colour.

Any underbody sealer requires regular inspection to make sure there are no loose flakes. If this is evident scrape off the loose area and remove any rust as described in the last paragraph. Apply a coat of red oxide cellulose primer surfacer and allow to dry. Underbody sealer is available in a brush on form, although when applied fresh at the garage it is sprayed on. A tin of this should be obtained and brushed on using a 2 inch paintbrush. On the wheel arches it is recommended that two coats are applied because of stones being thrown up by the tyres. Allow time for drying between each coat.

Finally, before lowering the car to the ground again, check the exhaust system for leaks with the engine running. Take care not to allow the engine to run for too long otherwise there may be an accumulation of exhaust fumes under the car.

Car cleaning - exterior

It is recommended that once a week the exterior of the car be washed and wiped dry. For this job a flexibrush on the end of the garden hose is best, a sponge to assist wiping down and a leather to finish the operation off.

First make sure that all windows and doors are closed. Thoroughly wet the car with water using a gentle spray. Take care not to aim the jet of water direction at the windows or radiator grille. Once the dirt has been loosened wipe down the panels using the brush with water still running through it as this way the paintwork should not be scratched by road grit.

Next apply wax car shampoo or a little non-detergent washing up liquid, working from the roof downwards. Any stubborn dead flies, marks or tar may be removed using white spirit on a soft cloth. Do not forget to clean the wing mirrors, front grille, the wiper blades and, of course, the wheels with the hub caps removed. A leather must not be used with a detergent or shampoo as it will cause it to rot.

Finally rinse off all the suds with plenty of clean water and wipe dry using a leather. Wipe all spots and smears from the windscreen, rear screen and door glass may be polished with a rag soaked in a methylated spirits and water solution. Chromium plating requires regular cleaning with a damp cloth or leather. Occasionally one of the special polishes for chromium plating may be used but on no account use an ordinary metal polish.

Every six months it is recommended that the exterior be wax polished. There are, however, several important points to be noted before polish is used on a car.

If the car is new do not polish for at least two months to allow the paint to dry fully and harden.

If part of the paintwork has been re-sprayed treat as if new.

Do not use a 'cutting' paste to remove the dull film from cars sprayed with a metallic paint.

When purchasing a wax polish always make sure that it is suitable for the type of paintwork on the car.

Do not attempt to wax polish a car in the sun or when the body is still warm, having been in the sun. It will bake on and have to be removed with petrol.

Do not wax polish a car which has just been washed because paintwork absorbs moisture slightly and the wax coating can hold this moisture so giving an effect called 'micro blistering' caused by minute rust spots under the paint film.

Finally a few 'don'ts' to avoid deterioration of the paintwork:

Don't dust down or polish a dusty car. Always wash.

Don't get polish or wax on any of the glass.

Don't neglect hidden parts of the doors when polishing.

Don't leave birdlime on the paintwork - it will cause stains.

Don't park under trees especially in the hot sun or when raining.

Don't use a cutting compound or haze remover on cars finished with an acrylic paint.

Don't use wax without cleaning the car first.

Bodywork - paint touch-up

On any modern car with an all steel body the greatest enemy of all is rust and this is most likely to start under the wings or along the sills because the road wheels will fling water, mud and grit onto the paint surface and it will only be a matter of time before the paint skin is penetrated and rusting starts.

It is for this reason that many new cars are given a thick coat of underseal, usually of a bituminous or rubber base, to guard against rusting. However, if this was the end of the story paint maintenance would be relatively simple but unfortunately it is not because chips appear at the front of the wings, along the outside of the wing panels and doors as well as the edges of the bonnet and boot lid. Whilst the car is being cleaned these chip marks will become evident and it is important that they are attended to immediately otherwise rusting will occur and spread so that what was once a small chip will gradually turn into a large area requiring a great deal more renovation work.

Touch-up paint is usually available in either touch-up pencil, tin with a little brush in the lid or aerosol form and may be obtained as a good match to the original body colour. It must, however, be realised that some paint colours are more stable than others. Due to the action of sunlight on an older car an exact match may be difficult unless a tin of touch-up paint is mixed by the paint department of your local Triumph garage to match the exact colour of your car.

Use a touch-up tin with brush incorporated in the lid for making good chips and very small scratches.

To prepare the surface for touching up first use a silicone solvent to remove all traces of polish which will not allow the paint to adhere properly. If there are signs of rusting or the paint beginning to lift use a sharp pen knife and carefully scrape away the loose paint and rust. Then neutralise the rust with a little Kurust and allow to dry. With a piece of rag soaked in methylated spirits wipe away the dry Kurust.

The prepared spot may now be touched in with the touch-up brush. Shake the tin vigorously for a few minutes to ensure that the paint is well mixed and withdraw the brush. Wipe the brush on the inside of the neck of the tin and then dip in the end of the brush until there is a little paint on its just sufficient to touch in the area concerned. Very carefully apply a thin coat of paint only to the area concerned and allow to dry thoroughly. Apply a further thin coat so as to build up the paint to the original paint thickness. This will take time and patience but with care the touch-up should be indistinguishable from the surrounding area.

If there is a scratch on the paintwork which has penetrated the top coat of paint and the red primer is showing through, the basic procedure is the same. First remove all traces of polish with a solvent and then with the knife lift off any loose paint. Neutralise any rust and finally touch in the scratch, preferably with one sweep of the brush. For this, a fine brush may be better than the brush provided with the tin. Build up the paint to the original paint thickness.

The edges of doors and boot lid seem to suffer very much and small areas of rust frequently appear. In this case an aerosol tin of primer and enamel top coat will be required. Again use the silicone solvent to remove any

polish from the area concerned. Rub down the paint around the area with a little wet or dry paper grade 400 until the area is smooth. As the name implies the paper can be used either dry or with water; the latter method tending to keep the grit of the paper clear of dust and also acts as a lubricant. Neutralise any rust with Kurust and when dry wipe with a piece of cloth soaked in methylated spirits.

Before spraying make sure the car is sheltered from wind and dust. Shake the aerosol tin of primer for a few minutes to ensure that there is no sediment in the bottom. If this is the first time that an aerosol tin is being used try it on a piece of metal such as an old tin to get the 'feel' of the spray and then proceed to spray the prepared surface. Remember the success of this work lies in the preparation. The smoother the prepared surface, the better will be the finish. Hold the jet about six inches away from the area to be sprayed and work from the centre outwards, keeping the centre moist and the outside lightly sprayed and dry.

When dry very lightly rub the primer with wet or dry paper to roughen up the surface and inspect the surface for blemishes caused by dust or bad preparation. Rectify any faults by rubbing down again and applying a further coat of primer. It is only when the surface under repair is perfect that the final top coat may be applied. Again experiment on a piece of metal, if this is your first time, and when you are confident apply the top coat to the primer. Remember it is like ordinary household painting - two thin coats are better than one thick coat.

Should runs occur it is an indication that either too much paint has been applied at one go or the nozzle was too near to the surface being sprayed. Rub down the area concerned and start again.

With all touching up, be it a small spot or a larger rusted area, allow the paint to dry thoroughly, at least overnight, and then use a little rubbing compound to blend in the edges of the paint and remove any dry spray.

If the rusted area is near to a piece of chrome trim there is no need to remove it but mask up the chrome trim with a little sellotape or proper masking tape. This may be removed once the paint is half dry leaving no paint overspray marks on the trim. Take care when sticking down the tape and use a knife to push the tape around any curved areas.

Should the scratch be only a minor one

without penetration through to the undercoat it may be removed using a rubbing compound, but take great care in its use. It may leave a light patch.

Bodywork - deep scratching, dent or crease removal

This type of repair requires a little more work but is well within the do-it-yourself motorists' capabilities, provided that care is taken and the job is not rushed. Again preparation is the secret to good results. The method of approach will depend on the location of the damage but in all cases if it is possible to push the dent or crease out from behind so much the better. This may mean removal of a piece of interior trim. Should, however, this present problems then do not worry too much unless the original shape can not be achieved (even with building up with a filler).

For safety reasons on this next operation wear a pair of goggles or glasses to protect the eyes. Using an electric sander with an abrasive disc on the rubber pad remove all the paint right down to the bare metal from the area surrounding the damage as well as the damaged area itself. Work the area until all traces of paint including undercoat and primer have been removed and an area of bare metal is obtained.

Next coat the area of bare metal with a special zinc primer such as Galvafroid primer to give additional protection against future corrosion as well as providing a key for the body filler. Allow to dry thoroughly.

The body filler must next be prepared according to the manufacturer's instructions. Usually these came in two parts, a tin of filler in paste form and a hardener. Read through the mixing instructions and when fully conversant mix only enough for immediate use to guard against waste. Most fillers are expensive to waste - once the hardener has been added the paste has a very limited working time of a few minutes. It is best to mix the hardener using a piece of plastic or very stiff cardboard on a piece of hardboard or plywood.

The filler should be applied to the damaged area and about one inch either side of it so as to allow for preparing the surface for final finishing. Do not, however, apply the filler to paintwork as it will not adhere properly. Carefully smooth the filler to the contour of the body panel, but do not try to work the filler once it has started to harden.

When the filler has hardened it should be rubbed down using a coarse wet or dry paper grade 120. Do not use an electric sander for this or subsequent operations as its action is too fierce. Carefully rub the surface smooth until the contour matches the rest of the panel and is also relatively smooth. Use the paper either wet or dry. Wash down the area being worked upon and inspect for imperfections and small air holes or areas requiring further building up. On flat panels use a sanding block but on curved areas just use the paper by itself.

Mix some more filler and apply where necessary to make good any defects found. When the filler is dry blend into the rest of the area using wet and dry paper.

Now using 280 grade paper wet rub down the complete area, taking care to blend the filler edges to the bare metal. This may take time but remember the preparation determines the quality of finish.

Wipe the complete area dry and inspect again for any blemishes. These must be rectified at this stage. With the palm of the hand 'feel' the surface for any high or low spots caused by over ambitious rubbing down and again rectify if evident.

When you are entirely satisfied that the area is perfect the next stage is to mask over any adjoining panels or chrome trim with sellotape or masking tape and newspaper.

Apply a coat of Galvafroid Primer to give a good key for the primer as well as giving additional rust protection. Allow to dry.

The primer may now be applied with a good quality paintbrush which will not moult. Paint the whole of the area under repair and allow to dry. Very lightly rub down the surface with 400 grade paper wet and inspect for any imperfections. Then wash down and allow the moisture to dry. Apply a second coat of primer and again lightly rub down and wash.

The repair is now ready for receiving the top coat. Holding the nozzle about six inches away from the surface spray behind any catches or fittings first and then work from the centre of the panel outwards until the repaired section of the panel is covered. Make sure that the part overlaps the existing paint by a couple of inches to allow for feathering and allow to dry. Lightly rub down the surface with 400 grade paper wet and allow to dry.

Now spray on a second top coat and if necessary a third coat until the depth of colour matches the original paintwork.

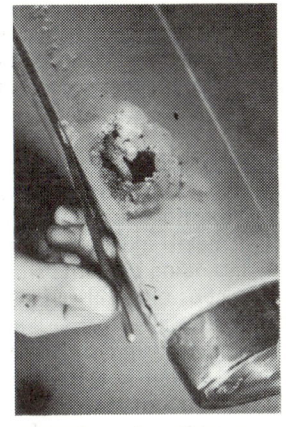

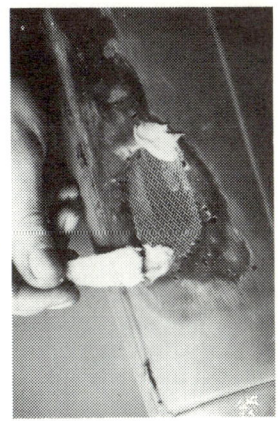

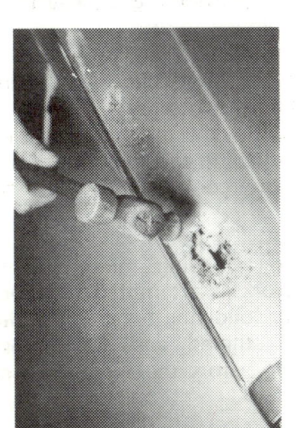

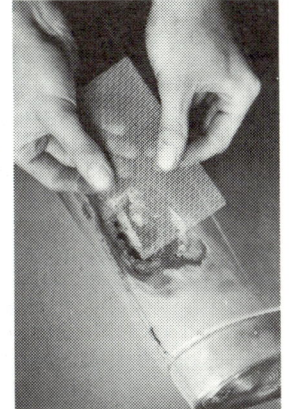

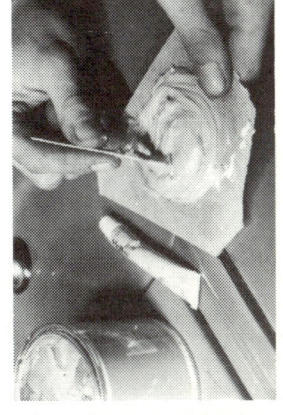

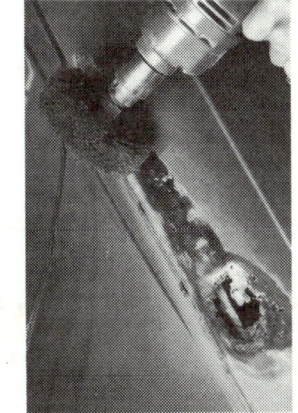

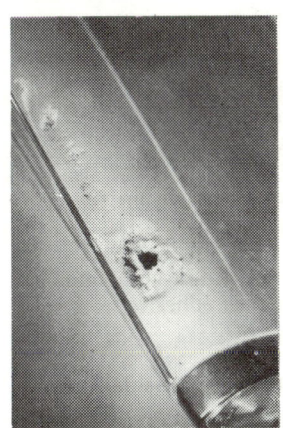

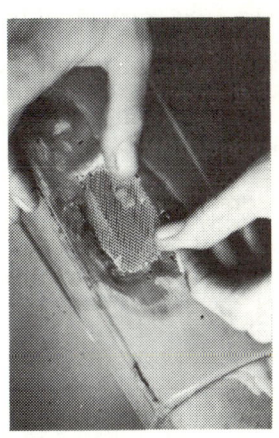

Minor body repairs sequence (1)

When the final coat is completely dry rub the surface with a soft cloth and some rubbing compound paying particular attention to the areas where the new paint overlaps the original. Wipe off the compound and inspect the finished result for signs of any blemishes which should be corrected by rubbing down and re-spraying.

Finally remove the masking tape and paper and lightly polish with a clean soft cloth. Do not apply a polish for at least two months to allow the paint to harden.

Provided that care was taken in the selection of materials and the instructions followed the results should be satisfactory but if something has gone wrong the following table should be of assistance.

FAULT	CAUSE
Blotchy finish	Insufficient number of primer or top coats
Paint runs	Spray nozzle too near panel during spraying. Too much paint applied
Rippling (called Orange Peel)	Too thick a coat application
Matt finish	Spray nozzle too far away from panel. Not all dust from previous flatting operation removed
Creasing	Unsuitable materials used for primer or top coat
Overspray	Insufficient masking - use cutting compound to remove it
Rough finish	Spraying in dusty or windy conditions
Faded patches of top coat (called Blooming) (Blooming)	Usually caused by spraying in damp conditions. Most pronounced with dark colours.

Bodywork - serious corrosion

Should a body panel such as a lower door panel, leading edge of a wing or sill as opposed to a main structural member be badly corroded it is within the capabilities of a more experienced do-it-yourself owner to make the panel look as good as new.

The first thing to do is to sand down the affected area for a further inspection. Do not forget to wear goggles or glasses to protect the eyes. Use an electric drill with sanding attachment and a coarse disc to remove the paint from the rusted section as well as the immediate area surrounding the more visible part affected.

Next hammer or cut away all affected metal until sound metal is reached and then treat with Galvafroid Primer paint to check subsequent corrosion.

Obtain a piece of perforated zinc plate as found in the old meat safes and cut off a section larger than the hole produced by the removal of affected metal and insert into the hole, if necessary, moulding it to the shape of the panel. Use paper clips or small self tapping screws to keep it in place.

Mix sufficient filler according to the maker's instructions to apply a thin coat to the zinc plate and immediate surrounding area and work it well in so as to provide a good key for subsequent layers. Allow it to dry.

Continue building up, a layer at a time, until the contour of the body panel has been reproduced and then allow to dry.

Thereafter follow the instructions given in the last section shaping and blending the filler to the existing body contour and finally paint.

Materials needed

Before any car cleaning, minor bodywork repair or paintwork is attempted it is recommended that the following list of possible requirements is studied and the necessary materials obtained before the operation is completed.

Car cleaning - interior
Vacuum cleaner
Carpet brush
Carpet shampoo
Upholstery cleaner
Soft soap (non-caustic)
Clean non-fluffy rags
Furniture polish
Small bottle methylated spirits
Small bottle paraffin
Jar Kurust
Seelastik flexible sealing compound
Bostik impact clear adhesive
Oil can

Car cleaning - exterior (underside)
Wire brush
Jar Kurust
Seelastik flexible sealing compound
Small bottle methylated spirits
Red oxide cellulose primer surfaces

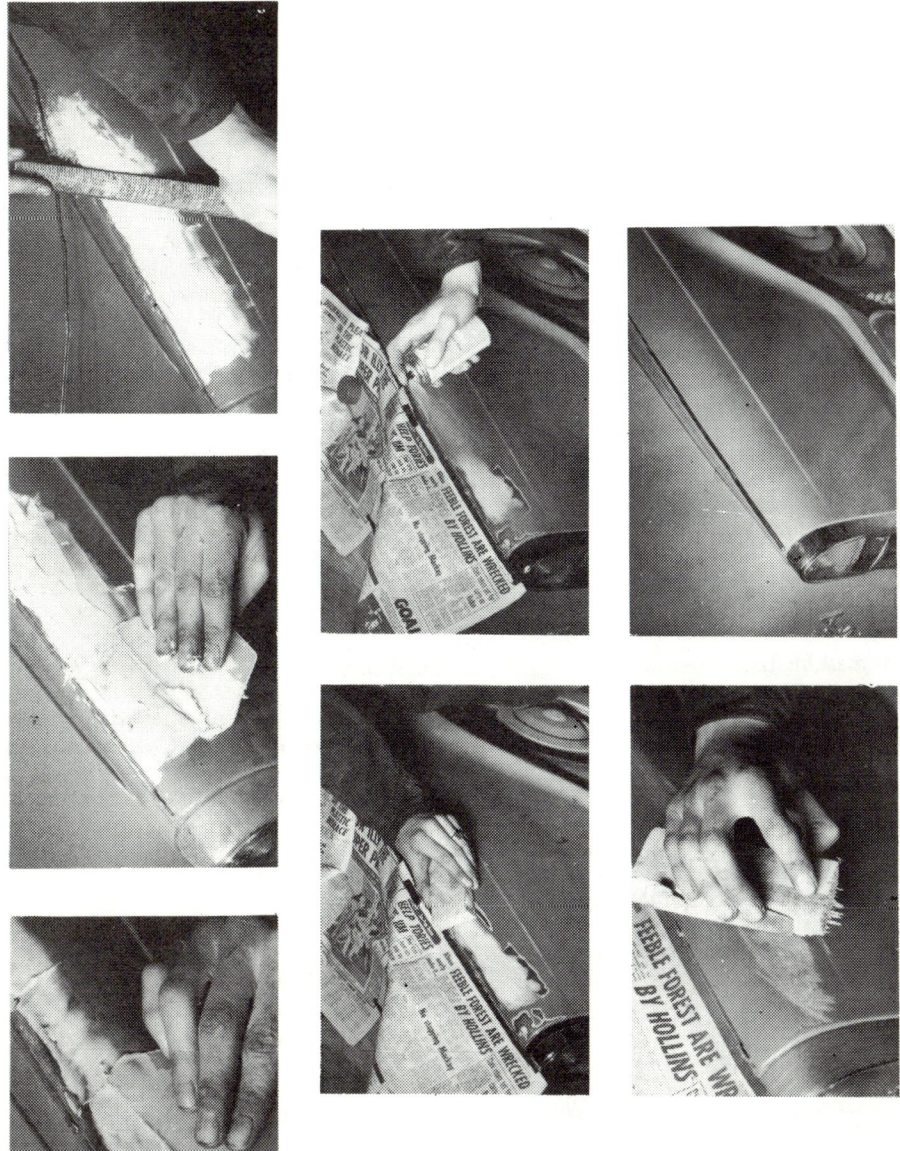

Minor body repairs sequence (2)

Holts car enamel spray (matching colour of car)
Tin brushing underbody sealer
Tin Holts 'Gun Gum'

Car cleaning - exterior
Hose and flexibrush
Car shampoo
Leather
Sponge
Piece of polythene sheeting about 3ft square
Bottle white spirit
Small bottle methylated spirits
Clean non-fluffy rag
Tin wax polish
Tin chrome plate cleaner

Bodywork - paint touch-up
Touch-up tin of matching enamel paint
Bottle silicone solvent
Jar Kurust
Small bottle methylated spirits
Wet or dry paper 400 grade
Touch-up paint - aerosol - primer
Touch-up paint - aerosol - matching enamel paint
Sellotape or masking tape
Newspaper
Belco rubbing compound

Bodywork - deep scratching, dent or crease removal
1 pair goggles
Electric sander with abrasive disc
Galvafroid Primer
1 pack Cataloy body filler
1 piece of plastic or hardboard (approx 3" x 2")
1 piece of hardboard or plywood (approx 1' x 1')
Wet or dry paper grade 120
Wet or dry paper grade 280
Wet or dry paper grade 400
1 tin brushing primer
1 good quality paintbrush
Holts car enamel spray (matching colour of car)
Holts car primer spray
Clean non-fluffy rag
Sellotape or masking tap
Newspaper
Belco rubbing compound

Bodywork - serious corrosion
Metal cutters
Perforated zinc plate
Plus all items mentioned in previous section.

Watch for rusting at points arrowed

Preparing your car for the MOT Test

All cars three years old or more are required by law to take an annual Ministry of Transport Test. This chapter has been incorporated in the handbook to help you to get your car through the test and therefore avoid the possible inconvenience and general annoyance that failing the MOT involves.

As the MOT test consists almost entirely of visual examination it is possible to carry out your own 'mini' MOT test at home before submitting the car for the test proper. If you carry out the checks, and providing the car has been regularly serviced as described in the Routine Maintenance chapter, there is no reason to suppose that your car will not pass the test.

Steering

With the car standing on level ground check the play on the steering wheel. It should move no more than three inches at its circumference before the wheels begin to move. Any more movement than this indicates excessive wear.

Open the bonnet and check the tightness and condition of the coupling at the lower end of the steering shaft. If this is worn it may well be the cause of some of the play at the wheel and must be renewed.

Apply the handbrake firmly, jack up the front of the car and from underneath check the tightness of the nuts on the U bolts which hold the rack and pinion steering gear to the front sub-frame.

While you are under the car inspect the rubber bellows at each end of the rack and pinion unit for tears or cracks and the resulting oil leakage. Should the bellows be damaged they should be renewed immediately as the loss of oil and the ingress of dirt will very quickly cause excessive wear to the rack and pinion.

With the car still jacked up rock the wheels in both the horizontal and vertical planes to check if there is excessive wear or free play in the wheel bearings. Also check to see if there is any movement in the upper and lower wishbone end ball joints. Any free play in the wheel bearings should be adjusted as described in Routine Maintenance.

Rest the car on stands or wooden blocks under the front crossmember, get under the car again and check the tightness of all the linkages in the steering mechanism and front suspension attachments. Check that all the nuts are tight and where applicable have their split pins correctly fitted. Excessive play or wear at any of these points may result in a test failure so this should be dealt with by the local garage before the car is submitted for a test.

Lower the car sufficiently for the tyre treads to rest on the ground and check the steering on full lock in both directions and make sure that the wheels do not foul the bodywork and chafe the tyres.

The degree of wear allowed in the steering gear is not laid down in precisely but it is up to the individual judgement of the tester as to whether he considers the car to be in a safe condition. Some testers may be more stringent than others but do not risk driving a car with faulty steering; always have worn parts replaced as a matter of course.

Brakes

Carefully examine all the metal and flexible hydraulic pipes and hoses for signs of leaking, corrosion and chafing. Clean off the mud and dirt from the flexible rubber hoses and examine them for any signs of perishing, bulging, wear caused by rubbing and age.

Check the brake drums and discs for any sign of hydraulic fluid leakage from the wheel cylinders or calipers. This form of leakage will severely affect braking efficiency when the car is road tested.

Get in the car, release the handbrake and depress the brake pedal. If there is excessive travel on the pedal before the brakes come on, the brakes will need adjusting. If there is evidence of sponginess in the pedal it will mean that air has entered the hydraulic system and the brakes will need bleeding. Brake bleeding

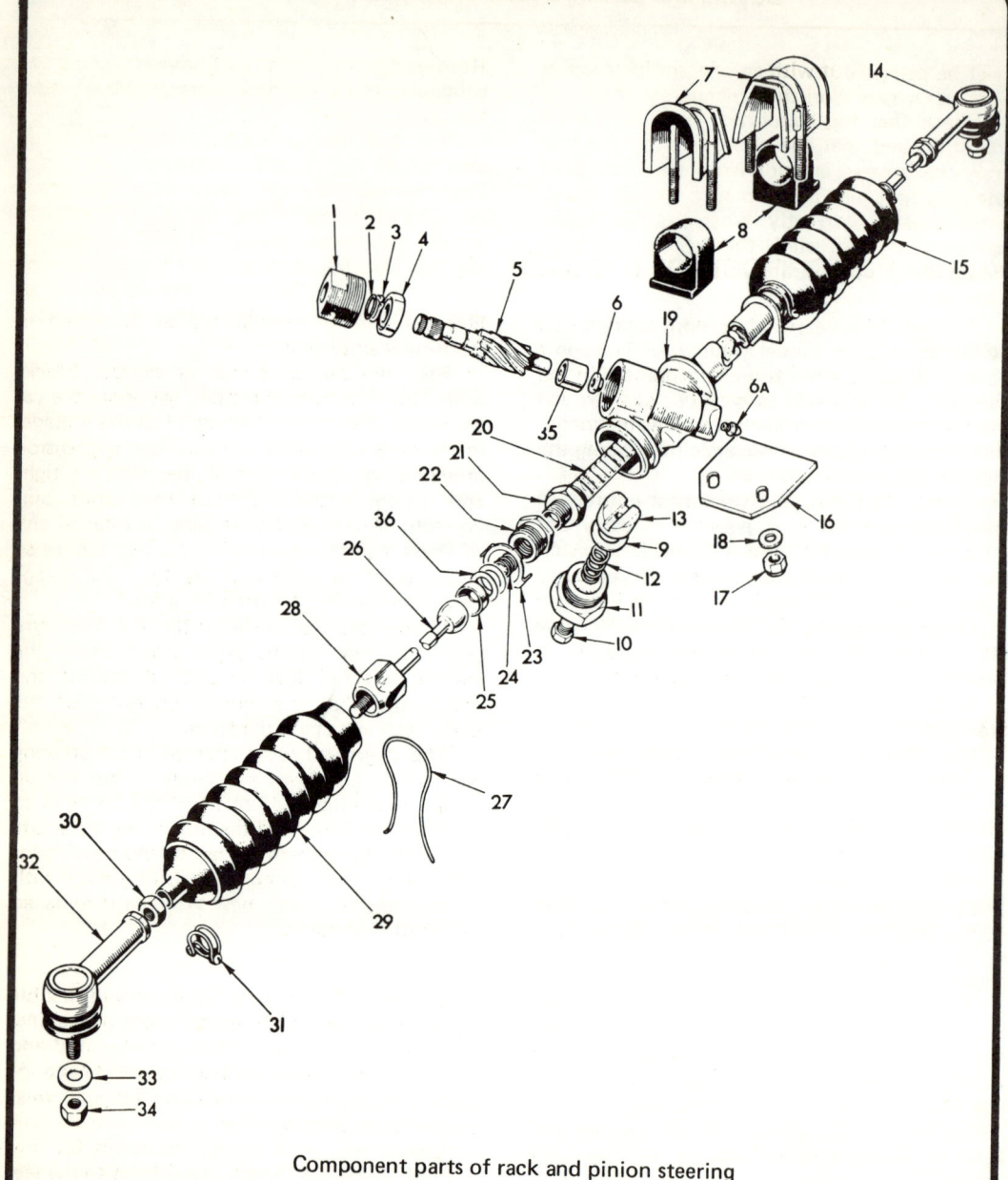

Component parts of rack and pinion steering

1 Retainer screwed	10 Plug grease	19 Rack tube	28 Cut nut
2 'O' ring seal	11 Cap nut	20 Rack	29 Rubber gaiter
3 Circlip	12 Spring	21 Locknut	30 Locknut
4 Ball bearing	13 Pressure pad	22 Sleeve nut	31 Wire clip
5 Pinion	14 Tie-rod end	23 Tabwasher	32 Tie-rod end
6 End cover	15 Rubber gaiter	24 Spring	33 Washer
6a Grease nipple	16 Locating plate	25 Thrust cup	34 Nyloc nut
7 'U' bolts	17 Nyloc nut	26 Tie-rod	35 Bush
8 Rubber bushes	18 Washer	27 Wire	36 Shims
9 Shims			

must be carried out with competent instruction from an Owners Workshop manual.

Check that the handbrake cable is in good condition and that the clevis pins on the rear brake backplates are not worn and that their retaining split pins are in place. Check handbrake operates correctly: When the rear brakes are correctly adjusted the handbrake lever should travel up the ratchet about four or five clicks before it is fully on.

Electrical

Switch on all the lights and check that they are all functioning correctly. Check the operation of the headlamps in the full beam and dipped positions. Also check that the headlamps are correctly adjusted and that the main beam warning light operates when the lights are on full beam.

Back the car up against a wall and check that the brake stop lights work both with and without the side lights on.

Check the operation of the indicator lights both front and rear. They should flash at between 50 and 120 times per minute.

Check that the lenses of the stop, brake and rear direction indicator lights are not broken or faded; they must show a clear colour.
1 Check that the horn operates properly and consistently. It must do so. Check the operation of the windscreen wipers - they must wipe properly and park in the correct position. Change the blades if streaking the windscreen. Then operate the windscreen washers - they must now work, effectively and easily.

Bodywork

If you are forced to submit a car with accident or corrosion damage for the MOT test, ensure that none of the damaged panels are jutting out or have jagged edges. Also ensure that corrosion or crash damaged panels and fitments are still securely fixed and are not liable to fall or break off the car when it is on the road.

The tester will examine the car thoroughly for excessive signs of rust and corrosion, particularly where the corrosion points may affect the safety of the car, such as front and rear suspension attachments, steering rack mounting point etc.

To inspect the underside of the car it is best to make use of a pit or ramps; if neither of these is available, jacking the car at the front and rear as each end is inspected will suffice.

Remember to give additional support to supplement the car jack before sliding under the car.

You will need a torch or inspection lamp, wire brush and a large screwdriver or chisel. Once beneath the car, clean away any heavy deposits of rust with the wire brush in order to inspect the metal beneath. If you suspect the rust has penetrated deeply into the metal, prod the worst affected areas with the screwdriver or chisel. Should the blade pass through the metal, it will be necessary to have a new section of underframe fitted or, if the damage is small and localised a metal plate welded over it.

Cover any areas that have been brushed down to the bare metal with red lead, aluminium paint or an underseal preparation, to prevent the further formation of rust.

Exhaust system

It should be fairly obvious if there is any fault in the exhaust system, as even the smallest of holes in the exhaust piping or silencer, or leak past a faulty joint, will cause the noise emitted from the exhaust to rise by many decibels. The only requirements for the MOT test are that the exhaust note should not be unduly loud and that none of the toxic exhaust fumes should escape from the exhaust system in such a way as to be able to enter the interior of the car.

If the exhaust system is leaking in one of its joints, the fault can usually be rectified by tightening the relevant clamp. Should the leak be caused by corrosion holes, the affected part should be renewed.

Road Test

The purpose of the tester driving the car on the road is to ensure himself that it handles correctly with regard to steering and brakes. If there is anything major wrong with the steering, you will probably already have spotted this fault and had it rectified before the test.

The tester will check the efficiency of the brakes by using a decelerometer, a piece of equipment which is not readily available to the public. However, you can do a rough test on the brakes using an ordinary brick. Drive the car onto a reasonably long, deserted straight and smooth stretch of road, place the brick on the passenger side floor on one of its narrow longer sides and gently accelerate up to 30 mph. Checking that it is safe to do so, apply the brakes hard without actually locking the wheels. The brick should fall over at this point quite quickly. Repeat the test and stop the car using the handbrake only; this time the brick should just topple over quite gently. If the car pulls violently to one side or other on heavy braking this may well cause failure of the test.

If all appears to be well the car can now be submitted for its test. Before taking it in make sure you have the log book and the old test certificate to hand for the tester. Have some petrol in the tank to enable the road test to be carried out.

It is advisable to leave instructions with the garage that any minor faults found should be put right on the spot to prevent a further waste of time and money. Any major faults should be confirmed before the repair work is begun.

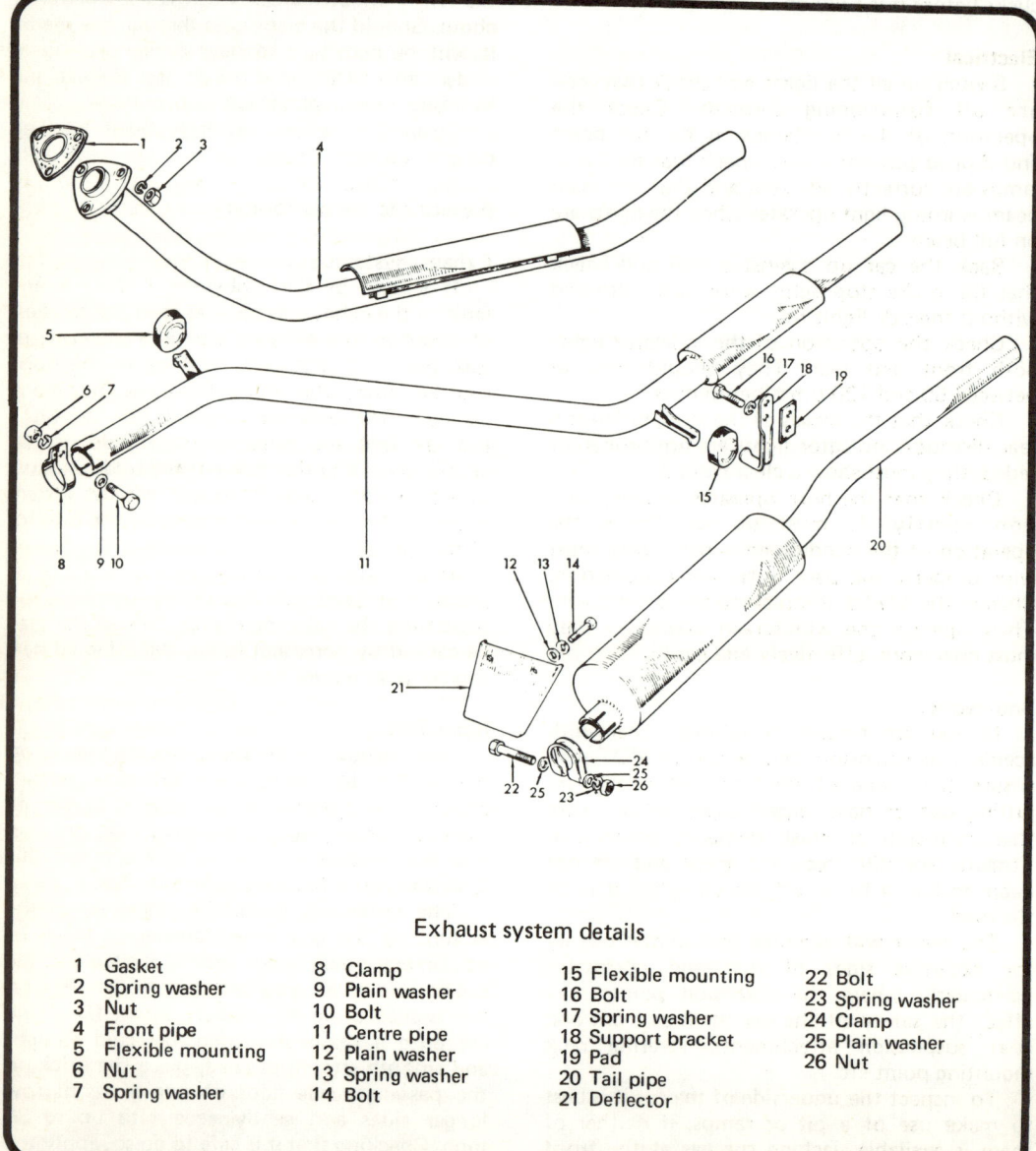

Exhaust system details

1	Gasket	8	Clamp	15	Flexible mounting	22	Bolt
2	Spring washer	9	Plain washer	16	Bolt	23	Spring washer
3	Nut	10	Bolt	17	Spring washer	24	Clamp
4	Front pipe	11	Centre pipe	18	Support bracket	25	Plain washer
5	Flexible mounting	12	Plain washer	19	Pad	26	Nut
6	Nut	13	Spring washer	20	Tail pipe		
7	Spring washer	14	Bolt	21	Deflector		

Buying and selling a used Triumph 1300/1500

Introduction

A car is the second most expensive purchase most people make in their lives. It is naturally important for those of you hoping to buy a used Triumph 1300 or 1500 that you obtain good value.

This chapter is designed to ensure that you do in fact buy a good car, even if your knowledge of cars and this type of transaction is very limited. If you study carefully these instructions you will find most of the faults in the car which you are contemplating buying and therefore will be able to calculate a reasonable price with regard to the condition of that vehicle.

It would have been very easy for the author to describe a perfect car and tell you to buy it when you find it. However, one fact must be stressed now. There is no such thing as the perfect car. Instead, the condition of used cars varies from scrap to immaculate, varying in price accordingly. Decide first upon the condition of the car of your choice and from that condition work out a fair price.

Listed are the three major categories and price ranges into which most used Triumph 1300 and 1500 models fall.

Category A (above average) — value: top book price.

The car must be in a first class condition throughout and be virtually unmarked. The mileage shown on the speedometer should average 12000 miles or less for each year of the car's life.

Maintenance of the car must have been regular and of a high standard. All parts of the car must be in good order, working correctly and not be in need of attention.

All tools as originally supplied with the car should be available and in good condition.

Category B (average) — Value: approximately 10% — 15% below top book price.

The car must be in reasonable condition and free from any major mechanical faults or severe body damage. All tools supplied by the manufacturer should be available and in reasonable condition. All parts must be functioning correctly and not be in need of immediate attention. The annual mileage should amount to no more than 16000.

Category C (below average) — Value: approximately 20% — 30% below top book price.

Cars in this category have been subjected to harsh usage, extra mileage and above average wear and tear — without regular maintenance. They should nevertheless be in a roadworthy condition.

If you wish to find the top book price for a particular car which is in 'A' Category condition, or accurate prices for cars in the other categories an excellent monthly publication is available to the public called, 'The Motorists Guide to New and Used Car Prices'.

It is a good idea to memorise the more important parts of this chapter before going to inspect a promising used car. As well as your good memory you will need a magnet! The reason for the latter will become obvious as you read through the chapter.

You will find it very much to your advantage to choose a time of day which will allow you at least one hour of good daylight to view the car. Try also to choose a dry day, as raindrops on the bodywork can cover a multitude of sins and give the paintwork a false appearance of high gloss.

When you first approach the car give no thought to the mechanical condition, instead concentrate on the body. Remember most mechanical assemblies can be renewed or repaired easily at a relatively low price compared with damaged or faulty bodywork.

Stand well back from the car and note any obvious faults, damage or repairs, such as areas of paintwork which do not match the rest of the car, rust, collision damage or badly finished body filling.

Next examine the bodywork and paintwork

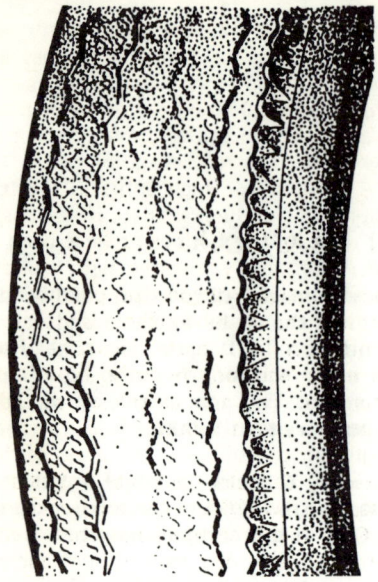

Over inflated

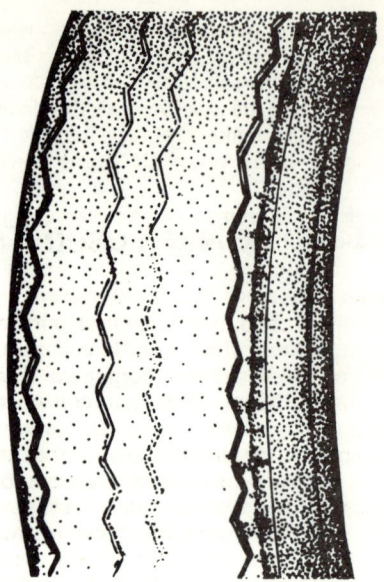

Under inflated

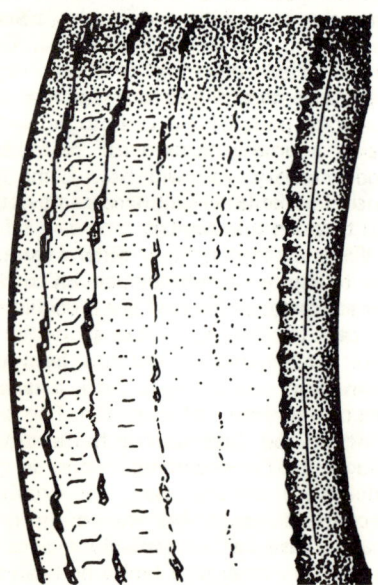

Excessive toe-in or toe-out

Illustrated are three examples of dangerous and illegal cross-ply Tyres. It is unnecessary for this type of excessive wear to take place. It is possible to rectify the causes of these types of wear early on if regular checking takes place. Consult your local Triumph garage if in doubt.

more closely. If the paintwork is well polished and clean, the chances are that the car has been well maintained, although this does not always apply — you would be surprised at the difference an expert can make the appearance of a shabby car given a few hours and some special materials!

If the paintwork seems to be in an unusually good condition for the year of the car, the car may have been resprayed. To check this, closely inspect the rubbers around the windows and chrome trim for small areas of overspray. If evidence of a respray is found, determine from the present owner the reason for this. Do not be too sceptical if he says it was to improve the appearance of dull or shabby original paintwork as resprays in a polyurethane type paint can be cheap and still provide an excellent finish. For this reason it is often worth giving a shabby car a quick 'blow over' rather than to spend hours restoring the original paintwork. Therefore, buying a resprayed car can often be to your advantage. You will have a car of above appearance for the same price as a car with original paintwork which will almost inevitably have faded.

Do not dismiss cars with paintwork which has a dull and powdery appearance. This is merely the result of neglect in the form of infrequent washing and polishing. With the price suitably adjusted, these cars can be good buys if the paintwork is intact.

Using a fine cutting paste such as 'T—Cut' or a chemical cleaner like 'Colour-Bak' neglected paintwork can often be brought back to a high gloss although this will take a considerable amount of time — a factor which should be taken into consideration.

Having established the condition of the paintwork it is time to find out what sort of shape the bodywork is in beneath it. Walk to the rear of the car and look along each side in turn. If the bodywork is rippled it is indicative of severe collision damage. Should the undulations extend the length of the car there is a good chance that the car is twisted. If you suspect that the car is twisted inspect the gap around each door. Each section of the gap should be uniform in width. Also note whether the doors are flush with their surrounding bodywork. It is possible that ill-fitting doors are the result of incorrect hinge and latch position adjustment. However, a combination of ill-fitting doors and rippled bodywork almost certainly points to a twisted body. A further

indication is uneven rear tyre wear.

If you suspect that the car has a twisted body ask the present owner if you can take the vehicle to a qualified garage to be placed on a jig and checked professionally for correct body alignment. If he refuses—go on home.

Any dents or high spots in the bodywork should be closely examined. If you suspect that any areas of the bodywork have been damaged and subsequently repaired with a plastic filler, place a magnet against the paintwork. Should the magnet not adhere there is at least 1/8 inch of plastic filler between the coat of paint and the metal skin of the body. Move the magnet around to find the extent of the filling and while you have the magnet out, run it along the length of the sills and the areas of front and rear wing between the wheel arches and doors. Also do a few random checks over the complete body to find any invisible repairs. Plastic filling in the sills or in the areas of front and rear wing between the wheel arches and doors probably means that rust has penetrated the metal in these parts; filling in other parts of the body points to accident damage.

When you have completed the bodywork inspection you must decide whether any faults found are acceptable and compatible with the price asked, before going further. Generally speaking repaired minor accident damage is acceptable—indeed you will be very lucky to find a car without a very slight amount of repaired damage. Cars with more extensive damage can be considered if the price is adjusted accordingly and if you are quite satisfied that the damage in no way affects the handling, performance, or general safety of the vehicle. Now rust: whether or not to buy a car which has started to rust is a difficult decision. It depends mainly upon the age of the vehicle.

As the Triumph 1300 has been in production since 1965 it is only reasonable to expect some degree of corrosion. This corrosion should only be superficial on the later produced cars, gradually becoming more serious for models of preceding years. The extent of rust acceptable depends entirely on the price and the age of the car but remember, once rust has got into the metal of a car body it can only get worse — there is no permanent cure.

Now inspect the chrome and bright metal exterior fittings. The chrome should have a high surface lustre with no signs of 'pickling' (spots of white corrosion) or of rust. Should the chrome have a bright finish and yet show signs of rust or corrosion spots, it has probably been recently cleaned with an abrasive chrome cleaner. Should this be the case, bear in mind the fact that the bright finish is only temporary, and, to retain it, regular abrasive cleaning and polishing will be required. When inspecting the chrome, also note the condition of the bumpers, hub caps and wheel rims. If any of these items have several small dents, and in the case of bumpers are bent or distorted, this is indicative of a careless owner — an attitude which may have affected the treatment of other parts of the car and the routine maintenance of the car.

Now turn your attention to the interior of the car. It should be clean and tidy with undamaged paintwork, headlining, seats, carpeting, door panels, door cappings and facia coverings. All mechanical items such as window winders, door locks, and seat adjusters should be working properly and easily. The interior of the car can give many clues as to the previous use of the vehicle. Examine the driver's seat for sagging or malfunctioning of the adjustment mechanism. If this fault is evident it indicates rough and careless usage or high mileage. Other indications of the latter are: heavily worn pedal rubbers, heavily worn carpeting or rubber matting where the driver's heels rest and bad nicotine stains on the headlining above the driver's seat. Should the condition of these items seem incompatible with the mileage recorded on the speedometer (which should work out at between 10 and 15000 miles per year if the car has had normal usage) look for a lubrication or air filter sticker of the type garages use, and see whether the mileage recorded on it tallies with the mileage shown by the speedometer.

When assessing the condition of the interior remember that seats, carpeting, headlining and paintwork which appear shabby but intact can be restored quite easily with a little work and the right materials, although some reduction should be allowed when calculating a fair price.

You have now inspected the paintwork, bodywork, chrome fittings and the interior of the car. Upon these four items depend the appearance of the car. 80% of the value of the vehicle depends on its appearance and the condition of the bodywork: Now is the time to decide whether or not it is worth proceeding further with the examination in the light of the considerations made so far in this chapter. If in your opinion the car still appears a good buy, it is time to check on the mechanical condition. This check will be mainly in the form of a test drive.

You must insist that the test drive is of at least fifteen minutes duration. This will allow the engine to reach its normal operating temperature, at which stage it is ready to 'divulge most of its secrets'. Sit in the driver's seat and if necessary operate the choke, then turn the ignition key to its first position. Note whether the ignition, oil pressure, choke and handbrake warning lights function. The lights give a valuable indication of the condition of their respective systems. Turn the key again, operating the starter motor, listen for a clunk as the starter engages the flywheel and a loud 'whurr' as it turns the engine over. The Triumph 1300 is normally noisy however. Either or both of these noises can mean heavy wear on the starter motor pinion or flywheel ring gear. Also note how fast the engine turns over on the starter. It is is sluggish, either the battery is heavily discharged or on its last legs. The engine should fire quickly and easily, although, should it prove difficult or sluggish in starting it is unlikely to be a serious fault. Probably a bad connection in the ignition circuit or incorrect adjustment of the points, plug gaps, ignition timing or carburettor(s). When the engine does fire note how quickly the ignition and oil pressure warning lights extinguish, also listen for a heavy clunking and/or rumble from the front of the car. If these noises are present they will probably disappear within a few seconds of the engine starting. The former indicates worn big ends and the latter, main bearing wear. If the oil pressure warning light goes out at the same time as the noises disappear it is safe to assume that a fairly high degree of crankshaft and associated bearing wear is present. Both are faults that can be expensive to repair. If both the ignition and oil warning lights extinguish at precisely the same time it is possible that they have been connected into the same circuit to hide a low oil pressure or a faulty charging system. This is quite a common trick.

Push the clutch pedal down and select first gear — the clutch pedal should have approximately 1 inch of free movement before it begins to disengage, any more than this indicates wear. The gear lever should be easy to move and should select the gear with little resistance. Let the clutch in slowly. The drive should be taken up firmly yet positively; there should be no shuddering or squeals. Note: If there is a loud report from the front of the car in the form of a sharp bang like a pistol shot it is indicative of serious wear in one or both of the drive shaft universal joints.

Once on the move use the first five minutes of the test drive to get used to the car and to allow the engine and gearbox to warm up before making any further decisions about its mechanical condition. When the first five minutes have passed and you feel fairly competent of driving this particular car pull into the roadside, noting how effective the brakes are and the distance the pedal travels before the brakes begin to operate. As with the clutch pedal the free movement should be about 1 inch. Should the pedal have more than 1 inch of free movement, try pumping the brakes. If this brings about an improvement there is air in the hydraulic system — a fault which should be rectified quickly if you buy the car. No improvement indicates that the brakes are worn or out of adjustment. Brakes that pull to one side or snatch are in need of immediate and probable costly attention. The fault could lie with the brake shoes or disc pads, the pistons in the hydraulic wheel cylinders or calipers, on the brake drums or discs. Before the car finally comes to rest, release the brake pedal and operate the handbrake. The car should stop quickly and efficiently; if not, either the handbrake is in need of adjustment or the rear brake shoes need renewing.

Draw away from the kerb and briskly accelerate through the gears. The movement from gear to gear should be easy and quiet, the acceleration smooth and unhesitant. A grating noise when changing gear with the clutch fully depressed is an indication that the synchromesh unit is worn, an expensive fault to remedy. Rough acceleration can be caused by one of many faults, however, the most likely are: inefficient and incorrectly adjusted ignition or an incorrectly adjusted carburettor.

Cruise along at about 50 mph, the level of noise from the engine, transmission and exhaust system should be low. The steering wheel should have less than 3 inches of free play before it turns the front wheels; (check that the column adjuster clamp is tight) also there should be no tendency for the car to pull to one side of the road unless the surface has a very steep camber, in which case a slight amount of pull towards the near side is acceptable. Sloppy steering and pulling to one side are

caused by wear in either the rack and pinion steering or ball joints, or by incorrect front wheel alignment. Drive the car through a series of bends and over a rough surface. Through the bends the car should seem surefooted and free of a lot of body roll, the steering light and precise. When on a rough road surface the car should feel solid and there should be few 'clonks' or rattles, also the steering should remain unaffected by the road surface. Loud 'clonks' usually indicate suspension wear or damage, whilst a tendency for the car to wander on a rough road is indicative, again, of steering gear ball joint and steering gear wear.

Next decelerate sharply from about 50 mph by progressively engaging lower gears and releasing the clutch pedal quickly as each gear is engaged. Try to avoid the owner's looks of consternation as you do so. If the selectors and synchromesh hub grooves are worn the transmission will probably jump out of third and second gears as each is engaged. Noisy and difficult selection of gears indicates heavy synchromesh wear, whilst a loud 'zizz' from the gear lever is caused by worn bushes and linkage. These faults can be expensive to repair.

Spend the next few minutes testing all the small items operated from inside the car: heater, horn, blower motor, windscreen wipers etc. Also note whether all the instruments are working correctly. A chat with the present owner about the car's history may also be beneficial.

On return to the outside do not switch the engine off, instead allow it to tick over. Open the bonnet and carefully listen to the engine — ask the owner to rev it up whilst you are listening. Generally speaking knocking noises from the lower half of the crankcase indicate a difficult and expensive repair, whilst light metallic tapping noises from the rocker cover suggests the valve clearances are in need of adjustment — an easy task to rectify. Squeaking noises may be caused by incorrect fan belt tension or worn bearings in the generator/alternator or water pump, the two latter usually necessitating replacement of the unit.

Generally inspect the engine and transmission as far as it is visible and ancillary components for oil, petrol, or water leaks. Try to determine the cause of the leak and estimate the cost of a repair. Oil dripping from the clutch area may indicate a worn crankshaft seal in the engine.

Examine the top of the battery: heavy

sulphate deposits indicate the battery has not been well maintained. Also examine the battery compartment and clamp for corrosion.

Stand well back from the car and note whether it appears lower on one side than the other; this fault is indicative of worn or damaged suspension units. Take into account most cars are a little lower on the driver's side. Next test the condition of the dampers by bouncing the car at each corner. After each bounce the car should return to its normal ride position within one up-and-down movement. If the car continues to move up and down in decreasing amounts it means that the dampers are worn and need renewing.

Move to the front of the car and grasp each front wheel in turn, firmly at the top and bottom and try to rock them. If movement of more than 1/32 inch top and bottom occurs, either the wheel bearings are worn or more seriously the stub axle ball joints are worn. Renewal of the latter can be expensive.

Next examine the tyres, including the spare. To be legal they must have at least 1 mm of tread across their complete circumference and across three quarters of their width. All tyres should preferably be of the same type. NOTE: Radial tyres might add a little extra value to the car.

Lastly ensure that the car has a working jack and wheel nut wrench.

The examination of the car is now complete and if you have closely followed the advice in this chapter you should have found most of the faults in the car, both mechanical, electrical and bodywork. Now is the time to work out a reasonable price for the car, taking into account its appearance and faults.

As previously stated the value of the car depends mainly on the appearance of the interior and bodywork. Therefore start your calculations by working out the cost of the body repairs needed to make the appearance of the car better. When you make your calculations assume that the repairs will be done by a garage. In this way you will end up with a more realistic figure. When you reach a figure deduct it from the top 'book price' for the same model and year of car as the one you have examined. Next consider the mechanical condition of the car and again work out the price of repairs (on a garage basis) needed to bring the mechanical parts up to A1 standard. Deduct this figure from the previously calculated value.

You should now have a basic price. Add to this the value of extras, such as radial tyres, accessories, road tax etc.

Now compare the condition of the car and the price you have worked out, with those in the three used car categories listed at the beginning of this chapter. Adjust your price according to what you think is a fair compromise.

Suggest a price considerably lower than this to the seller and let the bargaining begin. With a little luck you will end up with a price acceptable to both parties and one which should be fairly close to the price you originally calculated. Do not allow the excitement of buying a 'new' car affect your good judgement when you are haggling over the price. The best way to obtain the car at a lower price is to have the money in cash and to produce it during the price haggling. This method will not usually work in a garage, where you must expect to pay a little 'over the odds' anyway. If you are buying the car on a credit sale basis you must expect to pay a price considerably higher than the one you have calculated.

Before handing over any money ask to see the present owners receipt for the car, or a note from the Finance Company giving him permission to sell it. Inspect the log book too, open it right out and ensure that it has not been stamped 'Insurance total payment made' or words to that effect. This means that the car is a rebuilt write-off. Even in excellent condition these cars are not worth more than 70% of the usual value. Also check that the engine and commission numbers given in the log book are identical to those on the car.

Lastly check that the MOT certificate is valid and applicable and also that the mileage shown on the certificate is reasonable with that shown on the speedometer. When you hand over the money ensure that you receive a signed receipt in exchange. If the seller asks for a receipt for the car write the works 'pending independent investigation' above your signature. This may help you to redeem your money if you find any undisclosed or serious faults in the car within a few days of buying it.

Finally if you pay by cheque do not be offended if the owner refuses to hand over the car until he has cashed the cheque. He too, is entitled to take precautions in the same way as you have done. In the instance of this happening do insist on taking the car log book as a security in exchange for the cheque.

Ensure that the car has a working jack and wheel nut wrench

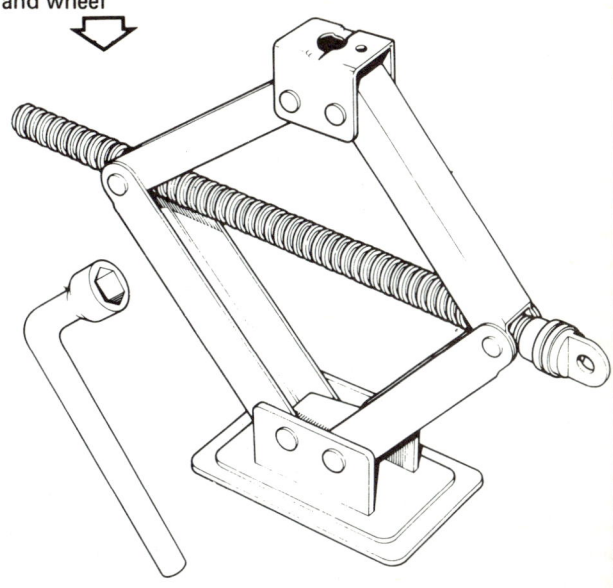

Checking for looseness in this manner can diagnose many worn parts in both the suspension and steering. It should never be overlooked.

Examine the spare tyre

Selling

Much of what has been said with regard to buying a used Triumph 1300/1500 is relevant in selling one, except, of course, that the boot is on the other foot.

Whatever the reasons are for selling, be they that you want a bigger, better or different car, you simply need the money, or your circumstances have changed, there is the relatively simple, standard approach - you want the best price for your car. With this end in view, whilst we hope that you will be giving value for money at the same time, there is a basic method of preparation for the car. Cleanliness is all. The cleaner the car, the higher the price. The bodywork's condition, both inside and out, should be the main selling point. Mechanical repair work is usually cheaper and faster to undertake than extensive bodywork repairs or renovation. The condition of the bodywork is usually indicative of the total condition of the car because it will show signs of age and disrepair sooner than the engine or gearbox, particularly on cars more than three years old. It is unlikely that owners will keep their cars in excellent condition mechanically and allow the body to drop off around it. Attend to the paintwork, chrome and all exterior trim, clean the outside thoroughly and polish the car, clean out the boot, and engine compartment and 'spring clean' the interior. There are methods of doing this explained in the Bodywork Chapter of this book. Because of the short time usually taken to actually complete a sale there can only be something less than a complete detailed check by a potential purchaser and rather more, a quick visual one.

As there are various ways of buying a used car so there are similar methods of selling but they are considered on their merits from completely different stand points. The way in which you sell your car will depend on why you are selling and these reasons were described in the first paragraph under Selling. The best prices are often obtained when part exchanging your car for a new one from an accredited dealer. However, shop around from dealer to dealer; their buying-in prices will vary according to how eager they are to sell the new car you want, and how eager they are to actually have your present car to re-sell. Nevertheless, with many dealers not wanting used cars of more than three years old it may be better to sell privately whatever your circumstances. Here, local papers, notice boards etc, are the best media for selling.

It is unlikely that you will receive the best price from a used car dealer at least as a cash transaction, unless he requires a good example for a particular customer, because he will have to put his mark-up onto the car to re-sell. Auctions do not often provide the best recompense. You can, of course, put on a reserve price. They usually do provide a sale, though, if you are finding it difficult to sell your particular car.

The same premise applies when you are selling your car as when you are buying one with regard to the actual selling price. The same guide is valid. However, there are other indications. Go around to various dealers and ask them for the prices of used cars of a similar age and condition to yours and look at the prices in the local papers, and then fix a reasonable price and be prepared to bargain. There are obviously price trends with regard to time and place to sell. Prices usually creep upwards in the spring and you may be fortunate to live in a high demand area such as London or eastern England where prices will again be marginally higher than elsewhere.

In conclusion remember when selling your car that the Law exists both to protect you and the buyer. The Trades Description Act does affect you as the seller. If the car you are selling is under a hire purchase agreement, the permission of the finance company must be obtained first. Irrespective of the age of your car it must have a current road fund licence, MOT certificate (when applicable) and insurance before it can even be tested on the road. Always give a receipt and do not part with the car and log book until you are sure you have the money if you are paid by cheque. Do not forget to make sure your name is removed from the log book and the buyer's inserted and that the local Taxation Office is informed of a change of ownership.

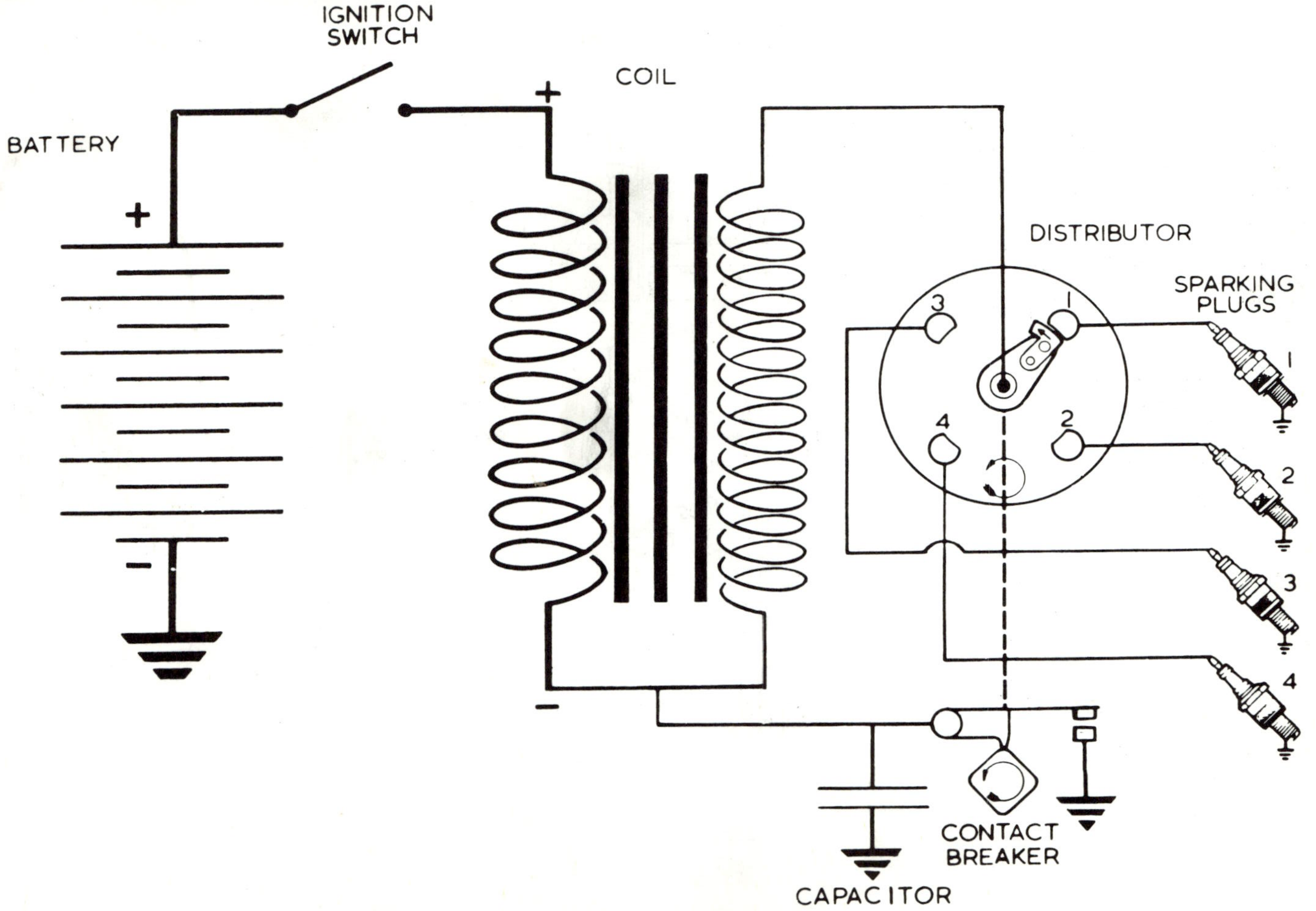
IGNITION SWITCH
COIL
BATTERY
+
+
-
-
DISTRIBUTOR
SPARKING PLUGS
1
2
3
4
1
2
3
4
CONTACT BREAKER
CAPACITOR

Circuit diagram - Ignition system
Note the 1 3 4 2 firing order of the spark plugs.

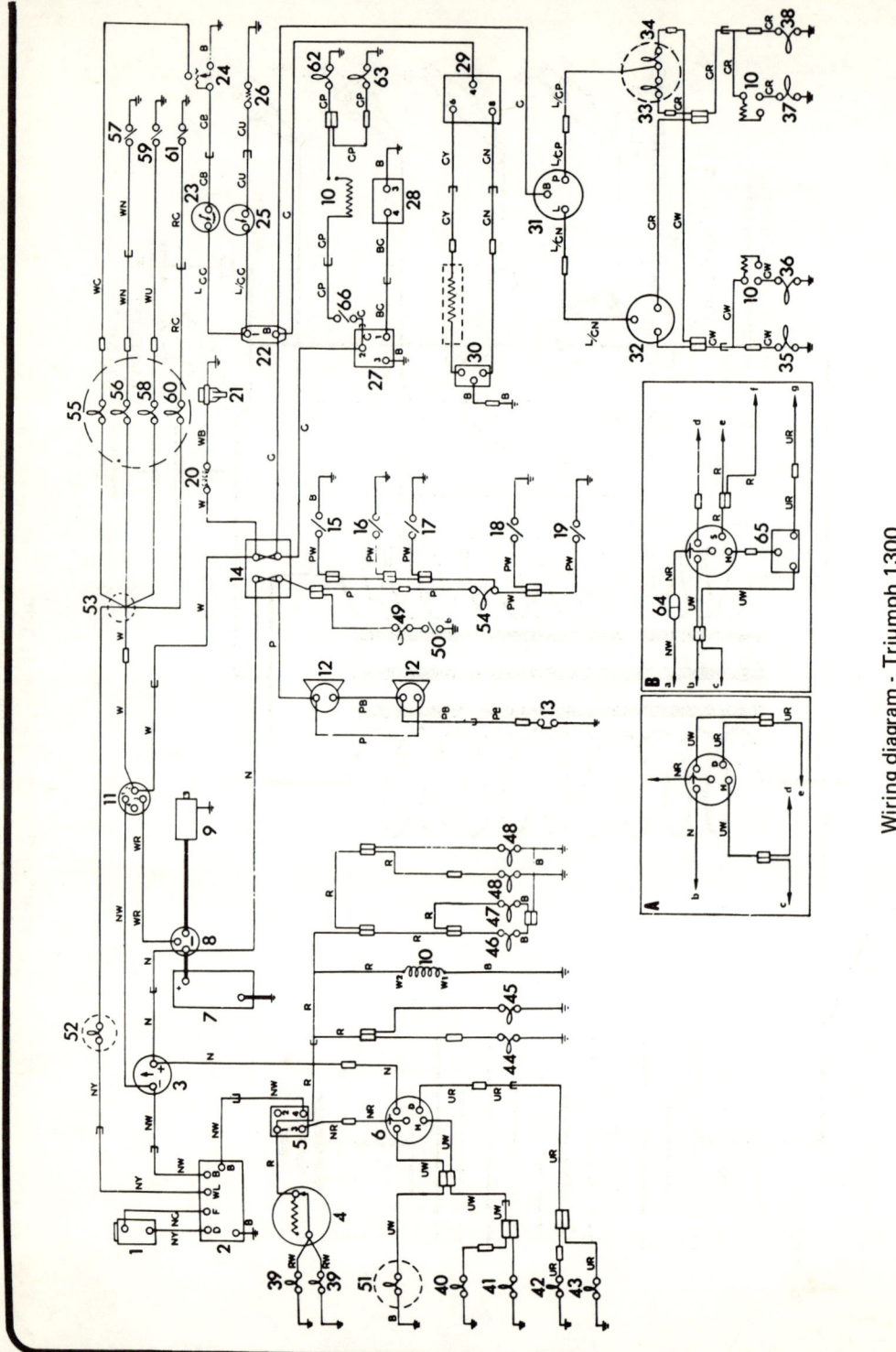

Wiring diagram - Triumph 1300

Key to wiring diagram - Triumph 1300

1 Generator
2 Control unit
3 Ammeter
4 Panel lamps rheostat
5 Master lighting switch
6 Column lighting and head-lamp flashing switch
7 Battery
8 Starter solenoid
9 Starter motor
10 Flasher dimming relay
11 Ignition switch
12 Horns
13 Horn push
14 Fuse unit
15 Interior light switch
16 R H front courtesy switch
17 R H rear courtesy switch
18 L H rear courtesy switch
19 L H front courtesy switch
20 Ignition coil
21 Distributor
22 Voltage stabilizer
23 Fuel gauge
24 Tank unit
25 Temperature gauge
26 Temperature transmitter
27 Windscreen wiper motor switch
28 Windscreen wiper motor switch

29 Heater blower motor switch
30 Heater blower motor
31 Flasher unit
32 Direction indicator switch
33 R H direction indicator warning lamp
34 L H direction indicator warning lamp
35 R H front direction indicator
36 R H rear direction indicator
37 L H rear direction indicator
38 L H front direction indicator
39 Panel lights (speedometer)
40 L H Main beam
41 R H main beam
42 L H dip beam
43 R H dip beam
44 L H side lamp
45 R H side lamp
46 L H rear lamp
47 R H rear lamp
48 Rear number plate lamp
49 Luggage compartment illumi-nation lamp
50 Luggage compartment illumi-nation switch
51 Main beam warning lamp
52 Ignition warning lamp
53 Warning lamp cluster
54 Interior lamp
55 Fuel warning lamp

56 Oil pressure warning lamp
57 Oil pressure warning lamp switch
58 Choke warning lamp
59 Choke warning lamp switch
60 Handbrake warning lamp
61 Handbrake warning lamp switch
62 L H stop lamp
63 R H stop lamp
64 "In line" Lucar connector
65 Foot dipswitch
66 Stop switch
A Dip beam flashing (for Italy only)
(a) Master lighting switch
(b) Ammeter
(c) Main beam warning lamp
(d) Main beam
(e) Dip beam
B Foot dip circuit (for N.A.D.A. only)
(a) Voltage regulator
(b) L H main beam
(c) R H main beam
(d) Ammeter
(e) Panel rheostat
(f) Side, front and rear lamps
(g) Dip beam

COLOUR CODE

N	Brown	LG	Light Green
U	Blue	W	White
R	Red	Y	Yellow
P	Purple	S	Slate
G	Green	B	Black

Key to wiring diagram - Triumph 1500

69

Key to wiring diagram - Triumph 1500

1 Alternator
2 Ignition warning light
3 Battery
4 Battery condition indicator
5 Ignition/starter switch
6 Radio supply — see 'Radio facility'
  page 38
7 Starter motor
8 Ballast resistor
9 Ignition coil — 6 volt
10 Ignition distributor
11 Connector block
12 Master light switch
13 Front parking lamp
14 Night dimming relay winding
15 Tail lamp
16 Plate illumination lamp
17 Panel rheostat
18 Instrument illumination
19 Cigar lighter illumination
20 Main/dip/flash switch
21 Dip beam

22 Main beam
23 Main beam warning light
24 Fuse
25 Horn switch
26 Horn
27 Cigar lighter
28 Luggage boot lamp
29 Luggage boot lamp switch
30 Roof lamp
31 Door switch
32 Voltage stabilizer
33 Fuel indicator
34 Fuel tank unit
35 Fuel warning light
36 Temperature indicator
37 Temperature transmitter
38 Windscreen wiper switch
39 Windscreen wiper motor
40 Stop lamp switch
41 Night dimming relay contacts
42 Stop lamp
43 Heater motor

44 Heater switch
45 Windscreen washer pump
46 Windscreen washer switch
47 Reverse lamp switch
48 Reverse lamp
49 Turn signal flasher unit
50 Turn signal switch
51 L.H. front flasher lamp
52 L.H. rear flasher lamp
53 L.H. turn signal warning light
54 R.H. front flasher lamp
55 R.H. rear flasher lamp
56 R.H. turn signal warning light
57 Oil pressure warning light
58 Oil pressure switch
59 Choke warning light
60 Choke switch
61 Handbrake warning light
62 Handbrake switch
63 Heated back-light switch
64 Heated back-light

COLOUR CODE

N Brown
U Blue
R Red
P Purple
G Green

LG Light Green
W White
Y Yellow
S Slate
B Black

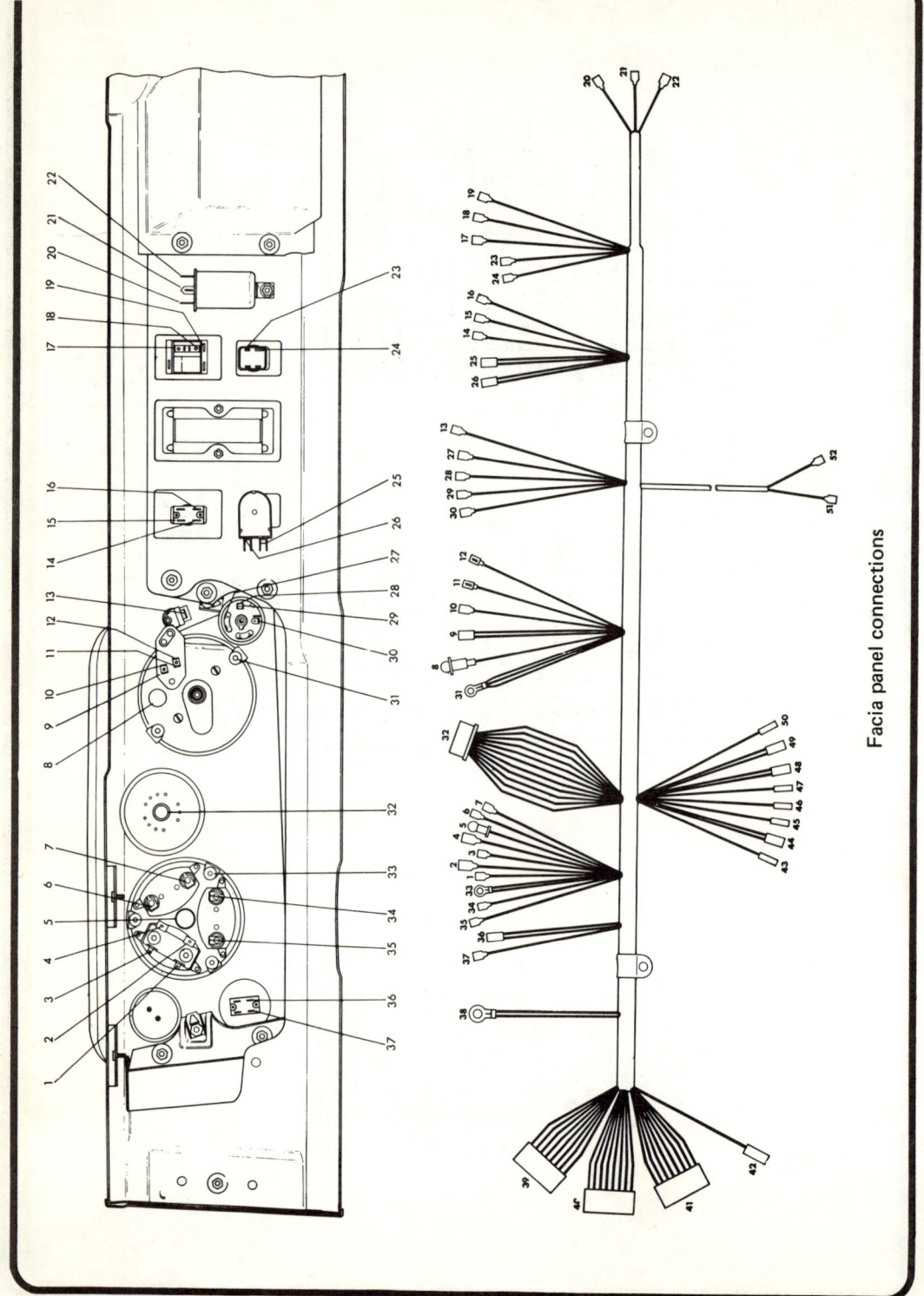

Facia panel connections

KEY TO FACIA PANEL CONNECTIONS

No.	Colour	Terminal End	Circuit
1	Brown	17 amp. Lucar & Cover	
2	Brown	35 amp. Lucar & cover	
3	Brown/white	17 amp. Lucar & cover	Ammeter
4	Brown/White (thick)	35 amp. Lucar & cover	
5	Red/White	'Push in' bulb holder	Gauge cluster illumination
6	Green/Blue	17 amp. Lucar & Cover	
7	Lt. Green/Green	17 amp. Lucar & cover	Speedo illumination
8	Red/White	'Snap in' bulb-holder	
9	Green (2)	17 amp. double Lucar & cover	Voltage stablizer
10	Green	17 amp. Lucar & Cover	
11	Lt. Green/Green	17 amp. Lucar	
12	Lt Green/Green	17 amp. Lucar	Choke w/light switch
13	White/Blue	17 amp. Lucar & cover	
14	Brown/Red	17 amp. Lucar & cover	Master lighting switch
15	Red	17 amp. Lucar & cover	
16	Brown/White	17 amp. Lucar & cover	
17	Green	17 amp. Lucar & cover	Heater blower switch
18	Green/Yellow	17 amp. Lucar & cover	
19	Green/Brown	17 amp. Lucar & cover	
20	Lt. Green/Brown	17 amp. Lucar & cover	Flasher unit
21	Lt. Green/Purple	17 amp. Lucar & cover	
22	Green	17 amp. Lucar & cover	
23	Black	17 amp. Lucar & cover	Interior lighting switch
24	Purple/White	17 amp. Lucar & cover	
25	Red/White (2)	17 amp. Lucar & cover	Instrument illumination rheostat switch
26	Red (2)	17 amp. Lucar & cover	
27	Brown/White	17 amp. Lucar & cover	
28	White	17 amp. Lucar & cover	Ignition/Starter switch
29	White (thick)	17 amp. Lucar & cover	
30	White/Red	17 amp. Lucar & cover	
31	Black (3)	Earthing tag washer	Speedo earth
32	Green/White White/Blue Red/Green Green/Red Lt. Green/Purple White/Green Brown/Yellow White Black Blue/White White/Brown	Warning light Cluster Socket	1 L.H.flasher w/1 2 Choke w/1 3 Handbrake w/1 5 R H flasher w/1 6 Flasher w/1 7 Fuel w/1 8 Ignition w/1 9 Supply 10 Earth 11 Main beam w/1 12 Oil pressure w/1 Gauge cluster
33	Black (2)	Earthing tag washer	
34	Lt. Green/Green	17 amp. Lucar & cover	Fuel gauge
35	Green/Black	17 amp. Lucar & cover	
36	Black (2)	17 amp. Lucar & cover	Windscreen Wiper switch
37	Black/Green	17 amp. Lucar & cover	
38	Black (2)	Earthing tag washer	Harness Earth
39	Black Green (Black sleeve) Green/Purple Brown	1 3 4 5 Lucar Multi Socket (Red)	Fuse box to voltage stabilizer Stop lamp switch to dimmer relay. Starter solenoid to ammeter.

No.	Colour	Terminal End	Circuit
	Red/Green	6	H/brake switch to warning light.
	Blue/White	7	Column switch to main beam filament.
		Lucar Multi Socket (Red)	
	Purple/Black	8	Horn switch to horns.
	Blue/Red	9	Columns switch to dip beam filament.
40	White/Red	2	Starter solenoid to switch.
	Green/Brown	3	Switch to heater blower motor.
	White/Brown	4	Oil pressure switch to warning light.
	Green/Red	5	D.I. switch to L.H. flashers.
	Green/Black	6 Lucar Multi Socket (Black)	Tank unit to fuel gauge.
	Green/Yellow	7	Switch to heater blower motor.
	Green/Blue	8	Temp. transmitter to gauge.
	White	9	Ignition switch to coil.
41	White/Green	1	Fuel tank unit to warning light.
	Brown/White	2	Master lighting switch supply.
	Brown/White	3	Ammeter to control box.
	Green	5 Lucar Multi Socket (White)	Stop lamp switch supply.
	Green/White	6	D.I. switch to R.H. flashers.
	Red	7	Master light switch to side lamps.
	Black/Green	8	W/screen wiper motor to switch.
	Brown/Yellow	9	Control box to ignition warning light.
42	Purple/White	Bullet & double snap	Interior lighting.
43	Purple/Black	Bullet and snap	*Horn switch.
44	Blue/White (2)	Double bullet & snap	*Headlamp main beam.
45	Blue/Red	Bullet and snap	*Headlamp dip beam.
46	Brown/Red	Bullet and snap	*Headlamp flasher supply.
47	Brown	Bullet and snap	*Lighting selector switch supply.
48	Green/Red (2)	Double bullet & snap	*Flashers , L.H.
49	Green/White (2)	Double bullet & snap	*Flashers, R.H.
50	Lt.Green/Brown	Bullet and snap	*Flasher switch-supply.
51	Green/Purple	17 amp. Lucar and cover	Stop lamp switch.
52	Green		

*Steering Column Switches.

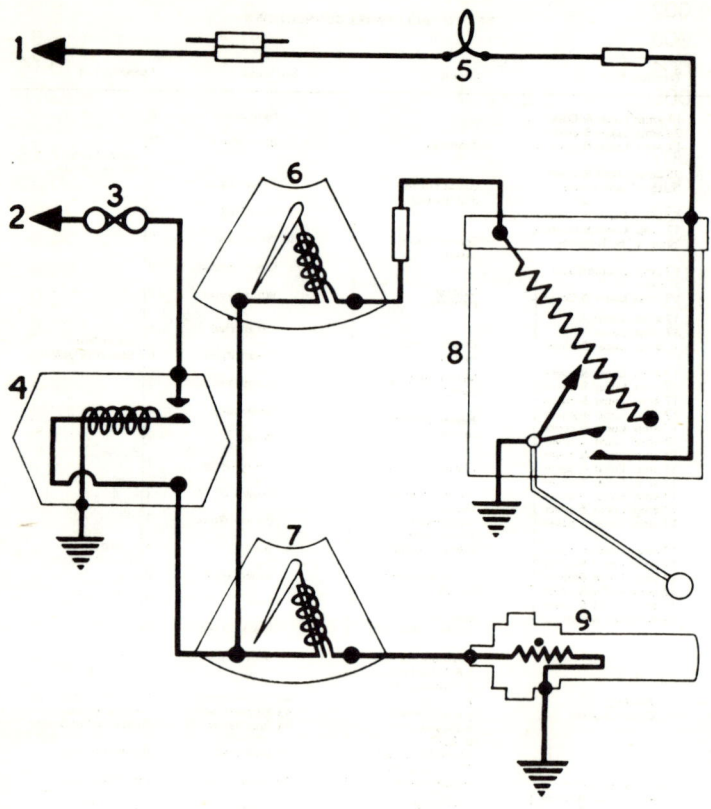

Fuel and temperature indicator wiring circuit

1	Feed cable	6	Fuel gauge
2	Feed cable	7	Water temperature gauge
3	Fuse	8	Fuel tank sender unit
4	Voltage stabiliser	9	Thermal transmitter
5	Warning light		

Metric Conversion Tables

Inches	Millimetres	Inches	Millimetres
0.001	0.0254	0.1	2.54
0.002	0.0508	0.2	5.08
0.003	0.0762	0.3	7.62
0.004	0.1016	0.4	10.16
0.005	0.1270	0.5	12.70
0.006	0.1524	0.6	15.24
0.007	0.1778	0.7	17.78
0.008	0.2032	0.8	20.32
0.009	0.2286	0.9	22.96
0.01	0.254	1.0	25.4
0.02	0.508	2.0	50.8
0.03	0.762	3.0	76.2
0.04	1.016	4.0	101.6
0.05	1.270	5.0	127.0
0.06	1.524	6.0	152.4
0.07	1.778	7.0	177.8
0.08	2.032	8.0	203.2
0.09	2.286	9.0	228.6
		10.0	254.0

Torque Wrench Settings

lb ft	Kg m	Kg m	lb ft
1	0.138	1	7.233
2	0.276	2	14.466
3	0.414	3	21.699
4	0.553	4	28.932
5	0.691	5	36.165
6	0.829	6	43.398
7	0.967	7	50.631
8	1.106	8	57.864
9	1.244	9	65.097
10	1.382	10	72.330
20	2.765	20	144.660
30	4.147	30	216.990

Metric Conversion Table

Distance

Miles	Kilometres		Kilometres	Miles
1	1.61		1	0.62
2	3.22		2	1.24
3	4.83		3	1.86
4	6.44		4	2.49
5	8.05		5	3.11
6	9.66		6	3.73
7	11.27		7	4.35
8	12.88		8	4.97
9	14.48		9	5.59
10	16.09		10	6.21
20	32.19		20	12.43
30	48.28		30	18.64
40	64.37		40	24.85
50	80.47		50	31.07
60	96.56		60	37.28
70	112.65		70	43.50
80	128.75		80	49.71
90	144.84		90	55.92
100	160.93		100	62.14

Capacities

Pints	Litres	Litres	Pints	Gallons	Litres	Litres	Gallons
1	0.57	1	1.76	1	4.55	1	0.22
2	1.14	2	3.52	2	0.09	2	0.44
3	1.70	3	5.28	3	13.64	3	0.66
4	2.27	4	7.04	4	18.18	4	0.88
5	2.84	5	8.80	5	22.73	5	1.10
6	3.41	6	10.56	6	27.28	6	1.32
7	3.98	7	12.32	7	31.82	7	1.54
8	4.55	8	14.08	8	36.37	8	1.76
9	5.11	9	15.841	9	40.91	9	1.98
10	5.58	10	17.60	10	45.46	10	2.20
11	6.25	11	19.36	11	50.01	20	4.40
12	6.82	12	21.12	12	54.56	30	6.60

Metric Conversion Table

Tyre Pressures

lb/sq in	Kg/sq cm	Kg/sq cm	lb/sq in
1	0.07	1	14.22
2	0.14	2	28.50
3	0.21	3	42.67
4	0.28	4	56.89
5	0.35	5	71.12
6	0.42	6	85.34
7	0.49	7	99.56
8	0.56	8	113.79
9	0.63	9	128.00
10	0.70	10	142.23
20	1.41	20	284.47
30	2.11	30	426.70

Inches	Decimals	Millimetres
1/64	0.0156	0.3969
1/32	0.0313	0.7937
1/16	0.0625	1.5875
1/8	0.125	3.1750
3/16	0.1875	4.7625
1/4	0.25	6.3500
5/16	0.3125	7.9375
3/8	0.375	9.5250
7/16	0.4375	11.1125
1/2	0.5	12.7000
9/16	0.5625	14.2875
5/8	0.625	15.8750
11/16	0.6875	17.4625
3/4	0.75	19.0500
13/16	0.8125	20.6375
7/8	0.875	22.2250
15/16	0.9375	23.8125

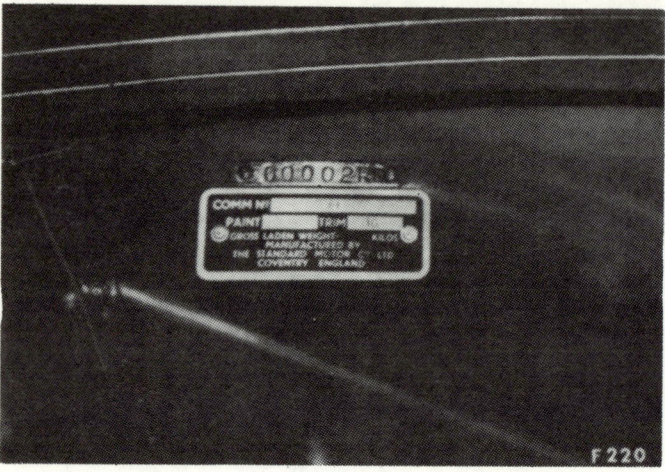

Identification plate

Always use the vehicle identification number
when ordering spare parts quoting the
Commission Number (Chassis Number), paint or
trim numbers, as applicable! These are
stamped on the plate attached to the top of
the left hand front wing valance as illustrated
above.

Fault finding charts

How to use the Fault Finding Charts

The fault finding charts have been specially written to help the Triumph 1300/1500 owner remedy certain situations which he may find himself in. We have imagined the driver sitting in the car faced with situations, such as the car will just not start in the morning or the steering starts to wander, and needing help. A logical step-by-step progression is made suggesting symptoms, then possible faults and a remedy. It has been our intention to try to get the car going if stopped or for the driver to keep motoring at least in knowledge of the fault which may be worrying him. We have re-stated how remedying tasks are done in many cases but we do assume that the driver has actually read the Routine Maintenance Chapter in his handbook and refer him to it in the less frustrating sections. Do not hesitate to turn from section to section to find the possible symptom straight away without always wading through from the beginning. Each section within a section is complete in itself.

THE CAR WILL NOT START, OR STOPS ON THE ROAD AND WILL NOT RE-START
Battery flat, starter motor faulty, ignition system at fault, no fuel reaching the engine

EMERGENCIES ON THE ROAD
Faulty lights or wiring, brakes useless, clutch fails

NOISES AND RATTLES
Rocker arm clearances, big end/main bearings, clutch squeal, brakes juddering, transmission judder, loose running components

GENERAL ENGINE FAULTS
Stalling and rough idle, lack of power and acceleration, engine misfires, engine pinking, excessive oil consumption, overheating, loss of coolant in the engine, warning lights do not go out, battery defective

OTHER MECHANICAL/ELECTRICAL FAULTS
Steering wander, clutch slip, stiff steering, defective light bulbs, spongy brakes, incorrect braking, tyre scuff and excessive wear

The car will not start or stops on the road and will not re-start

Symptom Ignition warning light fails to come on when ignition switched on

Possible Fault	Check and Remedy
Battery flat or leads loose. Ignition warning light faulty	Try the starter. If the engine fires the bulb is faulty. Change the ignition light bulb. If it does not fire check to see if headlights work. If not, clean and tighten down battery leads and check to see if lights then function and ignition warning light is on. If no lights, battery flat, recharge or replace.

Symptom Ignition warning light on but starter fails to turn engine

Possible Fault	Check and Remedy
Battery flat or loose leads	Check intensity of headlights. If dim battery needs charging. Car can be push or tow started. If lights bright check all battery, solenoid and starter motor leads for corrosion, cleanliness and tightness. (Not automatics).
Starter motor jammed	Turn the square head of the starter motor shaft with a spanner to free it, or place the car in a high gear and rock it to and fro to free the drive from the flywheel teeth.
Defective solenoid switch	Bridge the main terminals of the solenoid switch with a piece of heavy duty cable. If the starter motor functions the solenoid is defective and must be replaced.
Starter motor defective	If all the above methods fail to produce a result the starter motor must be defective and must be removed and repaired or replaced. However the car can still be push or tow started. (Not automatics).

Symptom Starter turns engine over slowly but with insufficient power to start it

Possible Fault	Check and Remedy
Battery flat or leads loose	Check battery, solenoid and starter motor leads for dirt, corrosion and tightness. If no improvement charge battery. Car can be push or tow started. (Not automatics).
Bad engine-to-chassis earth connection	Check condition and tightness of engine-to-chassis earth strap. If the battery fails to hold its charge under normal working conditions have the battery itself checked. If the battery is in good condition have the charging system similarly checked. If in bad condition replace the battery.

The car will not start or stops on the road and will not re-start

Possible Fault	Check and Remedy
Starter motor defective	If all the above fail to produce any improvement the starter motor is at fault and will have to be removed and repaired or replaced. The car can be push or tow started. (Not automatics).

Symptom Engine turns over normally but will not start or run

Possible Fault	Check and Remedy
Ignition system at fault (or no fuel reaching the induction of the engine)	Check that all the ignition leads are properly connected and dry. Remove one spark plug cap and that spark plug. Put the plug cap back onto the plug and turn the engine again and see if a spark will jump at the tip of the plug when earthed on the engine block. It should be quite visible. Replace that plug and its cap if the spark appears. Check that the distributor clamp bolt is tight and that the distributor cannot be moved easily. If it moves, reset the static ignition timing and retighten the clamp bolt. If all the above is correct and the engine still fails to fire it can be assumed that the fuel system is at fault. Go on to the next 'Check and Remedy' in order to trace the fault in the fuel system. If there is no spark at the plug lead remove the HT lead which comes from the coil at the centre of the distributor. Once again turn the engine on the starter and see if a spark can be obtained from this lead. If there is a spark the fault lies between the contact in the distributor cap and the plug. Check that the rotor arm is in good condition and making proper contact in the centre of the distributor cap and that the plug leads are properly attached to the cap. The four terminals inside the cap should be intact, clean and free from corrosion. If no spark comes from the coil HT lead, check next that the contact breaker points are clean and the gap is correct. This procedure is detailed in the 6000 service schedule. If there is still no spark obtainable it can be assumed that the fault lies in the low tension circuit. To check the low tension circuit effectively it is best to have a voltmeter of a 12 volt bulb in a holder with two leads attached. The procedure now given is arranged so that a break in the circuit, if any, can be found. Starting at the distributor, put one of the two leads from the tester (be it lamp or voltmeter) to the moving contact terminal and the other to earth. A reading (or light) indicates that there is no break in the circuit between the ignition switch and the contact points. Check that the condenser is in order by removing the distributor cap and rotor arm and rotating the engine until the points are fully closed — that is with the breaker arm resting between two high points on the cam. Switch on the ignition and with a non-conductive article such as a splinter of wood, move the contact points open by levering on the spring of the moving breaker. If there is a severe flashing spark it indicates that the condenser has probably failed whereas a mild spark is acceptable. An additional test to confirm condenser failure is to open the points by placing a piece of paper or fine cardboard between the contact points and disconnecting the condenser lead from the breaker terminal post. Then put your voltmeter or 12 volt bulb leads

The car will not start or stops on the road and will not re-start

between the terminal post and the condenser lead. With the ignition switched on, if there is a reading or a light, the condenser is faulty and must be replaced. To renew the condenser, detach the wire from the screw or terminal post, whichever applies, remove the mounting screw and replace the old unit with a new one. Check that the arcing has been virtually eliminated by carrying out the first test described. Once it is established that the condenser is satisfactory and there is still no spark it means that the coil is not delivering HT current to the distributor and therefore must be renewed. Returning to the low tension circuit, if there is no LT reading on the first check, repeat the test between the CB (−) terminal of the coil and earth. If a reading is now obtained there must be a break in the wire between the CB (−) terminal and the contact points. Renew the wire if this is the case. If there is no reading or light at this second check, repeat the test between the SW (+) terminal of the coil and earth. If this produces a reading or light then the LT post of the coil windings must be open-circuited and the coil must be replaced. If there is no reading or light at this third check there must be a break between the ignition switch and the coil. If this is the case, a temporary lead between the (+) terminals of the coil and battery will provide the means to start the engine until the fault can be put right.

No fuel reaching the engine

First check that there is petrol in the tank. If the gauge is suspect dip the tank with a clean piece of stick or wire. It must be clean to ensure that no dirt enters the fuel system.

Assuming that the tank has fuel in it next check that fuel is being supplied to the carburettor/s installation. Disconnect the fuel line at the float chamber and place a container under the open end of the pipe. A second person should now switch on the ignition and, as these models have a mechanical fuel pump, the starter motor should be operated. For safety reasons, so that no sparks occur, remove the HT lead from the centre of the coil. A good spurt of petrol should come from the fuel pump every second revolution of the engine.

If no fuel spurts out do not automatically assume that the pump is at fault but disconnect the fuel tank to fuel pump pipe at the pump inlet and blow down it to check that it is clear to the tank.

If it is clear hold a finger over the pump inlet and an assistant should turn the engine on the starter. If the pump is all right, a sucking should be felt on the finger as the vacuum operates in the pump. If this is not felt the pump is probably faulty and must be repaired or replaced. If suction is felt, it is possible that the pump is full of dirt thereby preventing it delivering fuel to the outlet pipe. To clean the pump, undo and remove the screw and lift off the cover, seal and filter. Clean the filter in petrol and remove any sediment with an old tooth-brush. Absorb petrol in the pumping chamber with a cloth and remove any accumulated sediment. Refit the outlet cover, seal and filter and secure with the screw. Should petrol be reaching the connection to the carburettor the next check should be to ensure that there is petrol in the carburettor float chamber/s.

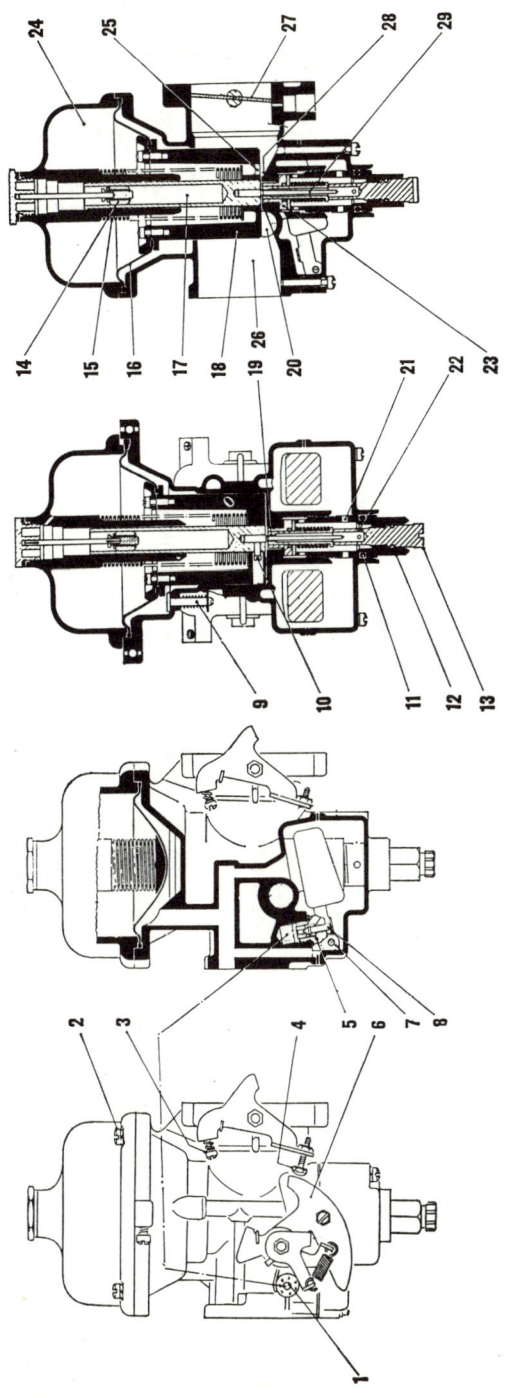

Cross section of Stromberg 150 CD Carburettor

1	Petrol inlet	6	Lever	11	'O' ring	16	Diaphragm	21	Inlet hole	26	Bore
2	Screws	7	Float arm	12	Jet assembly	17	Guide rod	22	Inlet hole	27	Throttle
3	Throttle stop screw	8	Needle	13	Jet adjusting screw	18	Air valve	23	Orifice bush	28	Bridge
4	Screw	9	Spring loaded pin	14	Damper	19	Jet orifice	24	Chamber	29	Metering needle
5	Needle seating	10	Locking screw	15	Coil spring	20	Starter bar	25	Air valve drilling		

The car will not start or stops on the road and will not re-start

S.U.Carburettor: Undo and remove the three float chamber cover retaining screws and check that there is petrol in the float chamber. If there is not it is probable that the needle valve in the cover is stuck closed.

Extract the float lever hinge pin and lift away the float from the chamber cover/s. Withdraw the needle from the valve body and make sure that it is free to move within the body. If it is stuck the condition is probably caused by dirt in which case it should be cleaned and reassembled.

Stromberg Carburettor: Take off the air cleaner and then remove the carburettor from the engine. Undo and remove the five screws that hold the float chamber to the base of the carburettor body. Check that the floats are free to pivot on the float spindle. Also check that the needle valve on the underside of the body is free in its holder. If it is stuck the condition is probably caused by dirt in which case it should be unscrewed, cleaned and refitted. It is very rare that dirt will stop the flow of petrol through the jet as it is of a comparatively large diameter. The easiest way to clean a blocked jet is to lower the jet by operating the choke control and attempt to start the engine with the hand over the air intake.

Providing the cleaning process has been done thoroughly, fuel should now reach and fill the float chamber. By this time it is quite possible for too much petrol to have found its way into the cylinders and that the plugs have become fouled or wet. It is wise therefore to remove the plugs and thoroughly clean them before attempting to start again.

If the engine fails to start after both the ignition system and the fuel system have been found to be in working order, it is likely that something of a more serious nature is wrong with the engine, such as a blown cylinder head or manifold gasket and a local garage should be consulted.

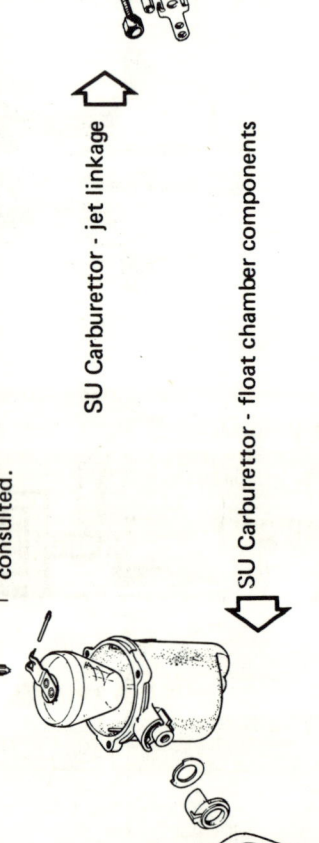

SU Carburettor - jet linkage

SU Carburettor - float chamber components

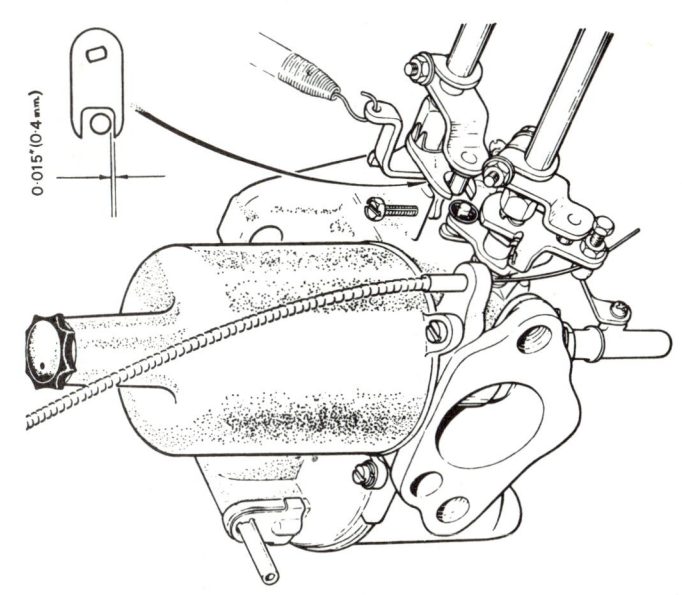

0·015" (0·4 mm.)

Carburettor fork lever adjustment

Twin carburettor installation

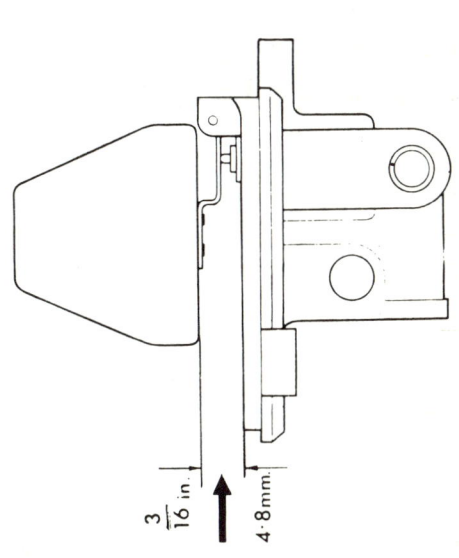

$\frac{3}{16}$ in.

4·8 mm.

Float height setting

Emergencies on the road

Symptom No lights come on at all when switch is operated but other electrical components work

Possible Fault	Check and Remedy
Faulty light switch or broken wire	Electrical faults of this type are very difficult to trace, particularly at night. Check that all visible leads to the head and tail lights and switch are intact. Be especially careful not to knock contacts when feeling for loose or hot wiring. Use the wiring diagram to help you identify the relevant wires but if you are in any doubt do not touch them as you may make final diagnosis and remedy more difficult. Call in a garage which should be able to fix at least a temporary repair. It is dangerous to proceed at night, even if very slowly, without lights.

Symptom Pedal travels right to the floor with little or no resistance and brakes are virtually useless

Possible Fault	Check and Remedy
Bad leak in hydraulic system resulting in considerable loss of fluid and no pressure being applied to wheel cylinders or master cylinder internal seals have failed	This fault is usually rather sudden and if you are lucky enough not to have hit anything, do not under any circumstances, attempt to drive the car any further. Apart from it being very dangerous you will be contravening the law. Check the slave cylinder hydraulic pipes and rubbers immediately for a hydraulic leak; if no leak is apparent then the master cylinder seals have failed. Call a breakdown vehicle and get the job done professionally making sure that the braking system is thoroughly tested after repair. Do not drive the car, there is no 'road-side' remedy.

Symptom Clutch fails to disengage when pedal fully depressed

Possible Fault	Check and Remedy
Hydraulic fluid leak	If moving push the gear lever into the neutral position and coast to a safe stopping point. Do not try to drive the car without a clutch. Check to see if there is an hydraulic leak caused by a loose union or fractured pipe. The most likely places for this to happen are either where it is attached to the master or slave cylinder. If the pipe proves to be broken call a garage for assistance.
Clutch disc sticking to pressure plate or release bearing very badly worn	If the clutch is found to be operating correctly and is properly adjusted one of these two faults may be apparent. These faults will almost invariably be associated with squeals and noises when the clutch pedal is operated. Check by stopping the engine, engaging a gear, depressing the clutch and putting on the handbrake. Then try to start the engine. If it refuses to turn, the clutch is stuck solid and must be removed and examined. If the engine

Emergencies on the road

is started without difficulty try using the clutch in the normal manner. If the drive continues to 'creep', a little when the pedal is fully depressed, carry on slipping the clutch for a few moments to try and rub off whatever may have been on the friction surfaces as a temporary measure. If no improvement of any kind results there must be a serious defect which will require examination of the clutch. This again is not an instant repair for obvious reasons.

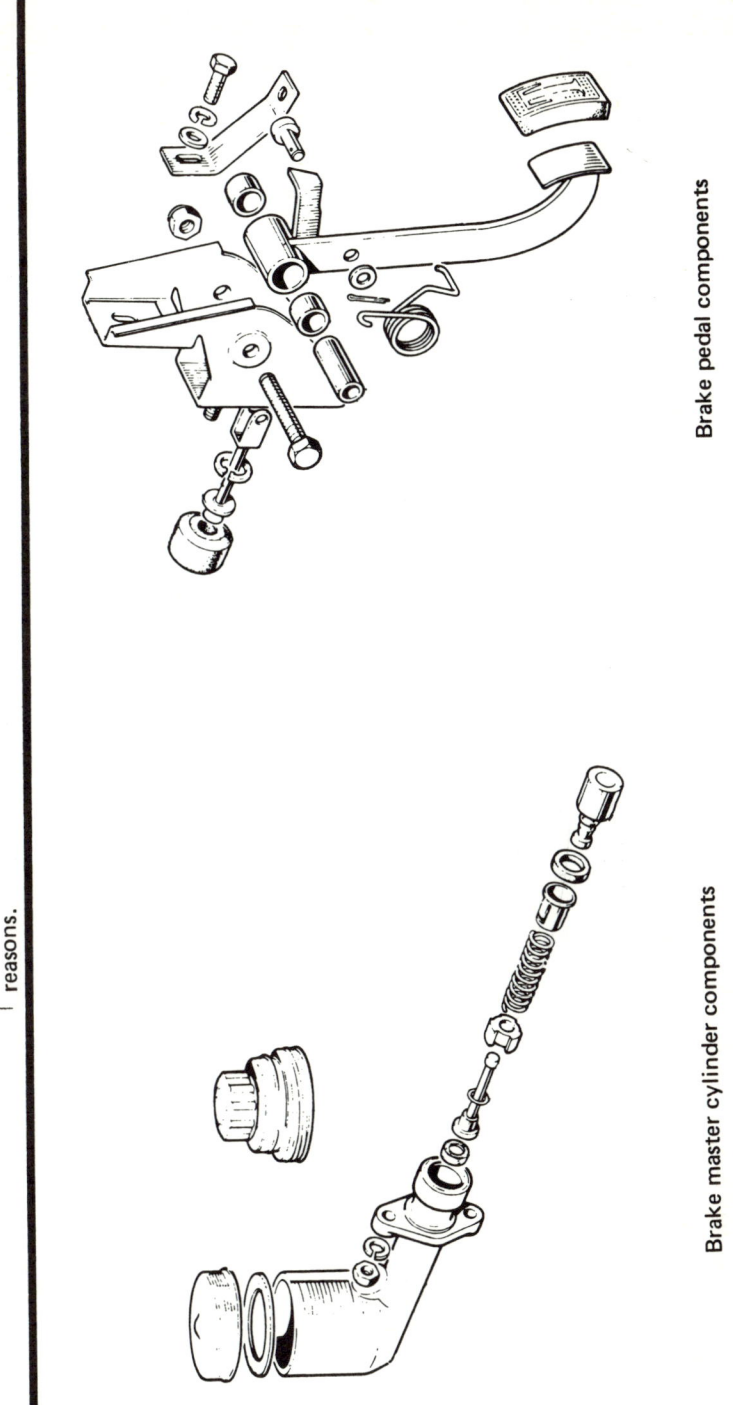

Brake pedal components

Brake master cylinder components

Noises and rattles

Symptom Excessive mechanical noise from engine

Possible Fault	Check and Remedy
Incorrect valve to rocker arm clearances	The noise associated with this fault is normally a tapping noise coming from the area of the rocker cover and is caused by one or more of the clearances being too great. To eliminate this noisiness, adjust the valve to rocker arm clearances as described in the 6000 mile service schedule.
Worn big end or main bearings	If the big end bearings are badly worn this will be noticeable by a heavy clunking from the engine once it has warmed up and will be particularly noticeable on deceleration. It may also be accompanied by lack of oil pressure, causing the oil warning light to stay on when idling. A worn main bearing will also cause loss of oil pressure in the same way, but rather than a clunking noise you will feel a heavy vibration from the engine.
Timing chain rattle	This is indicated by a metallic rattle and tinkling from the front of the engine and means that either the timing chain is worn badly or the tensioner is not functioning correctly.

Symptom Clutch squeal

Possible Fault	Check and Remedy
Clutch release bearing worn	Squealing noises from the clutch (and make sure they are from the clutch and not the fan belt or water pump) are most likely to come from a worn out clutch release bearing. The actual efficiency of the clutch may not be affected immediately but if the bearing is not repaired in good time the wear will increase and result in the clutch being operated unevenly. This will lead to excessive and uneven wear of the friction plate. Replacement of the clutch release bearing should be carried out by the local Triumph garage.

Symptom Brakes juddering

Possible Fault	Check and Remedy
Brake drums badly scored or warped	Remove and carefully examine the drums for signs of deep scoring. This can only have been caused by linings worn down to the rivets or to some foreign body, such as a piece of stone, finding its way into the drum. If there is no sign of scoring the drums may have become warped due to over-heating. This is not easy to see with the naked eye and should be checked by an expert with the proper equipment. A badly scored drum can be reconditioned, but this will probably be just as expensive as buying a new one, and certainly more expensive

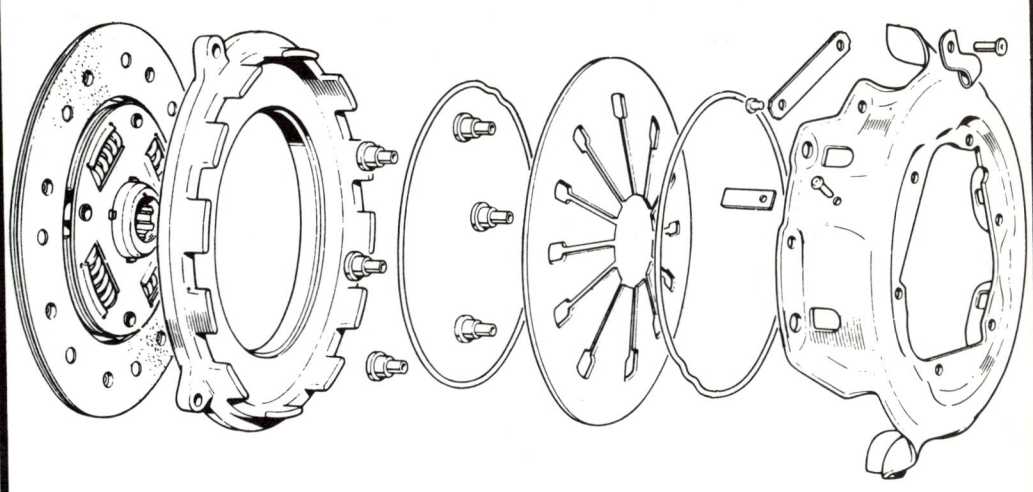

Clutch assembly components

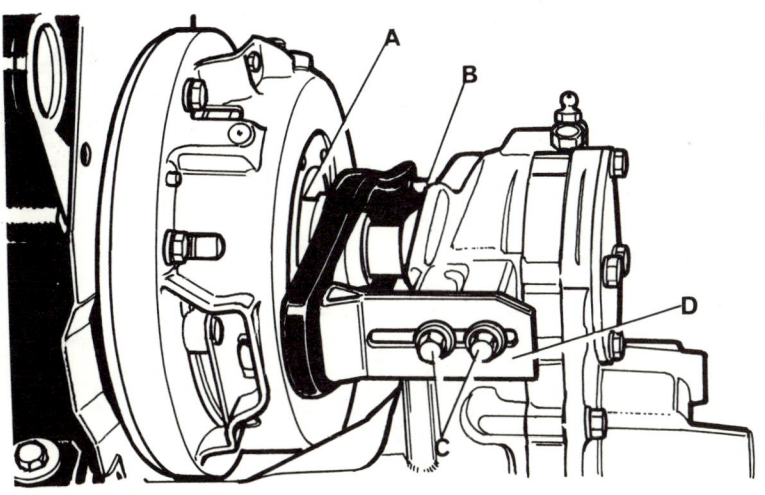

Clutch release assembly

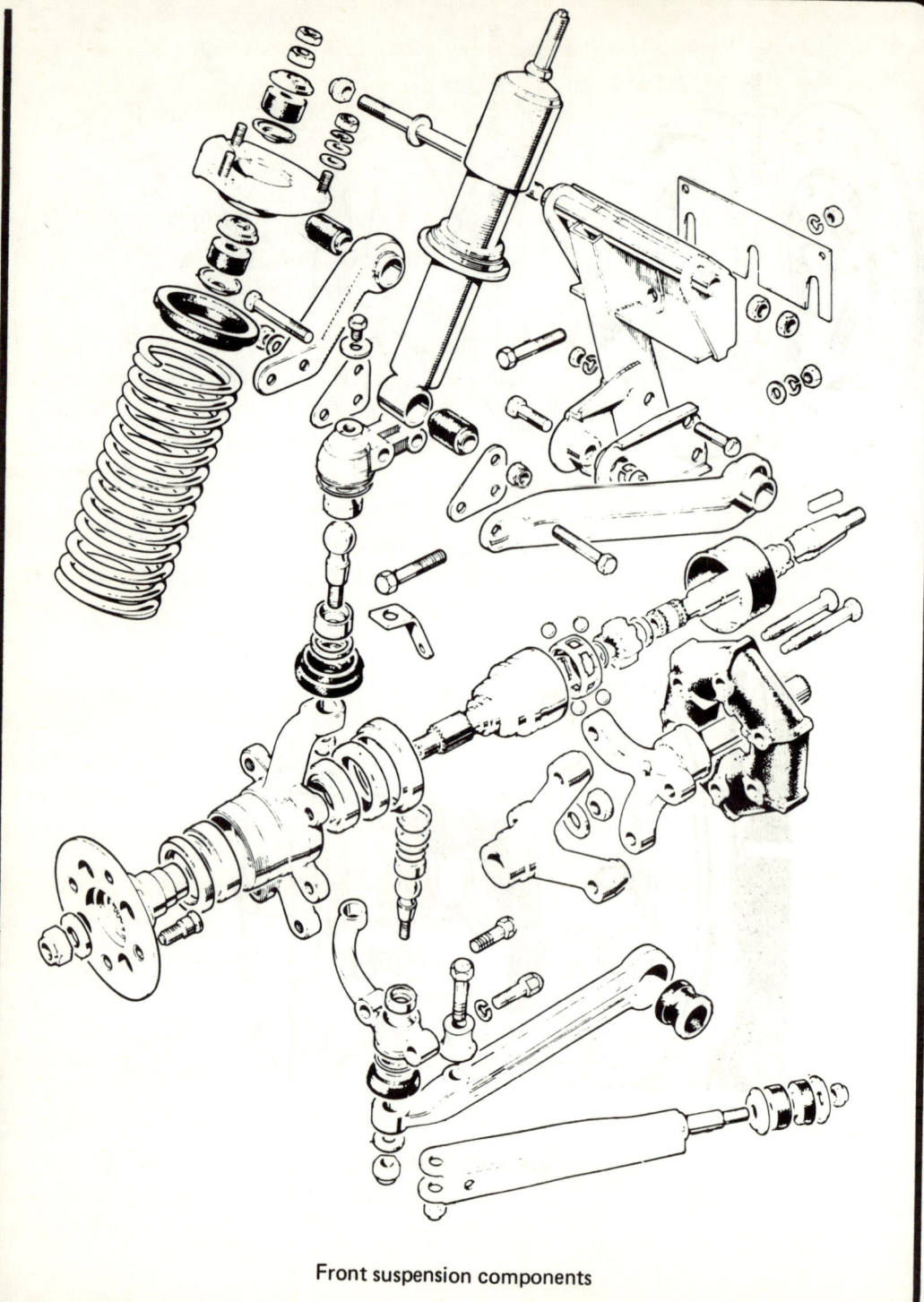

Front suspension components

Noises and rattles

than a good secondhand drum from a breakers yard. Warped drums cannot be reconditioned and should be replaced as a matter of course.

In the case of models with disc brakes on the front, examine the pads and the discs for signs of deep scoring. If there is no scoring it is possible that the disc may have become warped due to a knock or over-heating thereby causing excessive 'run-out' as it is called. Have this checked by an expert with proper dial gauge equipment and renewed if necessary.

Symptom Transmission judder

Possible Fault	Check and Remedy
Loose engine/gearbox mountings, worn universal joints, worn crownwheel or pinion, loose suspension mounting points, clutch snatching	The fault is very often associated with the clutch but not necessarily caused by any clutch defect. The fault is normally particularly noticeable when moving away from rest. Check first that the mountings are secure. Check the drive shaft constant velocity joints and rotoflex couplings by trying to turn the shaft with one hand. Inspect the rotoflex coupling for signs of oil contamination or deterioration. Excess movement indicates considerable wear, which could easily cause juddering. If worn, the old worn constant velocity joint or rotoflex coupling will have to be replaced. If they appear to be in order check the final drive gears by rotating the drive shafts. If there is a great deal of free movement before the drive takes up, the fault could lie here. Another indication of a worn crownwheel and pinion is a very noticeable 'clunk' on taking up the drive. Check also that the front and rear suspension units are securely mounted on the car body frame. If diagnosis indicates that the judder is due to a clutch fault it will be caused by 'snatching' between the friction surfaces and may be associated with other clutch faults already covered.

General engine faults

Symptom Engine stalls when idling or has very rough idle

Possible Fault	Check and Remedy
Idling speed set too low	Reset the carburettor idle speed adjustment on the carburettor as described in Service Operation 11.
Dirty or blocked air cleaner	Check and clean the air cleaner as described in the 6000 mile service schedule.
Choke stuck in operation	Check that the choke has not been left out and also that the cable is free and the choke releases correctly on the carburettor.
Air leak causing weak mixture	Check that the carburettor is tight on its mounting and that there are no signs of cracks round the inlet manifold. If a crack is found it can temporarily be sealed with PVC tape or similar material but a professional repair will have to be carried out very soon.
Dirty plugs or incorrect gap	Remove the plugs, clean them thoroughly and re-set the plug gaps to 0.025 in. (0.64 mm).
Contact breaker points dirty, incorrectly set or worn	Thoroughly check the points as described in the 6000 mile service schedule.

Symptom Engine suffers from lack of power and acceleration

Possible Fault	Check and Remedy
Air cleaner dirty or blocked	Check and clean air cleaner as described in the 6000 mile service schedule.
Incorrect setting of points. Worn points	Check and adjust points as described in the 6000 mile service schedule.
Accelerator linkage out of adjustment	Check that full travel of the pedal gives full travel of the accelerator linkage at the carburettor.
Insufficient fuel reaching the engine	Thoroughly clean the carburettor and jets as described earlier in this chart.

Some sample spark plugs

(Spark plugs can often give a reasonable indication of general engine condition
but only after the engine has run)

Plug too hot - white deposits

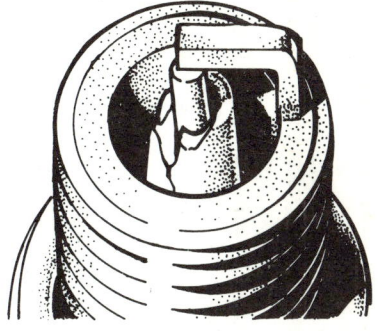

A chipped electrode

Typical damage caused possibly by pre-ignition

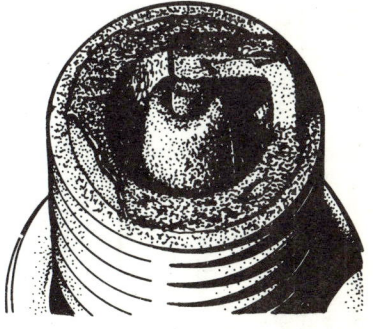

Plug too cold - dry black deposits

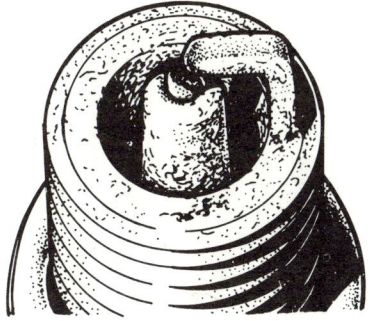

Badly burnt electrode

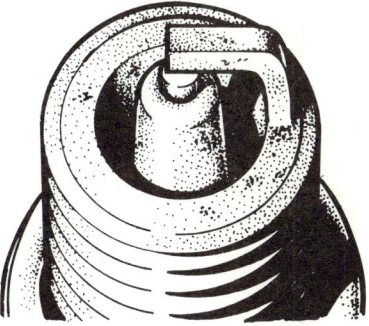

A good plug with light tan deposits

General engine faults

Possible Fault	Check and Remedy
Valve clearances incorrect	Check and adjust the valve to rocker arm clearances as described in the 6000 mile service schedule. This is not a fault that is easily diagnosed. Take your car to your local dealer for a proper check.
Automatic advance in distributor incorrect	
Engine compression low due to burnt valves	Once again this will have to be properly checked by your local garage. If the valves are burnt, the cylinder head will have to be removed and the valves reground.

Symptom Engine misfires at higher revs

Possible Fault	Check and Remedy
Loose or corroded electrical contacts in ignition system	Check, clean and tighten down all connections on the battery, coil and distributor. Check the condition of all leads. If they are cracked or damaged replace them as they may well be shorting under certain conditions.
Spark plugs dirty, gaps incorrect or plugs need replacement	Remove the plugs, clean them thoroughly and examine them for signs of damage. The Figure on Page 91 shows various faults that may occur. If all is well re-gap the plugs and replace them.
Points dirty, burnt or gap incorrectly set	Thoroughly check over the points and adjust the gap if necessary as described in the 6000 mile service schedule.
Dirt or water in carburettor	Clean the carburettor and blow out the jets to remove all sediment and dirt as described earlier in this chart.
Air cleaner blocked or dirty	Service the air cleaner as described in the 6000 mile service schedule.
Valve clearances incorrect	Check and re-adjust the valve stem to rocker arm clearances as described in the 6000 mile service schedule.

Symptom Engine 'pinks' under acceleration

Possible Fault	Check and Remedy
Too low octane fuel being used	On next fill up use one star higher grade of fuel and check to see if this eliminates 'pinking'. To get the timing absolutely 'spot on' it is advisable to have this checked by an expert with proper equipment. Excessive pinking puts a severe strain on the engine and will in the end cause considerable wear and damage. If the pinking still persists the ignition is probably

General engine faults

too far advanced. By loosening off the distributor clamp bolt at its base and gently rotating the distributor in an anticlockwise direction the ignition can be retarded a degree or so to reduce the 'pinking'. Take great care not to retard the ignition too far as the car may cease to run altogether. Once a satisfactory result has been achieved, tighten down the clamp bolt, taking care not to move the timing setting at this point. Have the timing properly set-up as soon as possible.

Faulty automatic advance mechanism — This fault will only become apparent when the ignition timing has been correctly set. The remedy of it is best left to your local garage.

Pre-ignition due to engine overheating — Check cooling system for signs of overheating and remedy fault as detailed later in this chart.

Pre-ignition due to excessive carbon deposits in combustion chamber — Take your car to your local garage and discuss the advisability of decarbonising.

Symptom Engine suffers from excessive oil consumption

Possible Fault	Check and Remedy
Oil leaks from crankshaft rear oil seal, timing cover gasket and oil seal, rocker cover gasket, oil filter oil seal, sump gasket, sump drain plug washer	Have a really good check round having cleaned off the engine. If oil is sprayed about try to identify where the oil is coming from. If it is identified as coming from the oil filter seal, rocker cover gasket or the sump drain plug, these are easily rectifiable. Simply replace the suspect gaskets, as shown in the service procedures on oil changing and valve clearance adjustments in the 6000 mile service schedule. If the leaks are from any of the other sources it would be advisable to consult your local garage.
Worn or broken piston rings or worn cylinder bores resulting in oil being burnt by the engine	This fault is nearly always indicated by a smoky exhaust system and a black, very sooty exhaust pipe. You must consult your local garage as soon as this becomes apparent or further damage may result. You will have to fit new rings or rebore the cylinders and fit new pistons depending on the degree of wear found on dismantling the engine.
Worn valve guides and/or defective valve stem seals	A lot of smoke blowing out from round the oil filler cap will indicate that oil is being burnt in the valve guides or the seals are ineffective. With a fault of this nature you should consult

General engine faults

Symptom Engine overheats when running under normal conditions

Possible Fault	Check and Remedy
Lack or loss of coolant	your local garage immediately. If coolant is boiling, switch off the engine and wait for some ten minutes until it has stopped. Then carefully remove the radiator cap with a large rag. As the system is under pressure the hot coolant may shoot out and if care is not taken a nasty burn could result. Whilst waiting for things to cool down a bit have a good look round all hoses, hose connections, drain taps, the radiator and the heater for signs of a leak. A leak is very often apparent by signs of rust water or anti-freeze but this can be misleading if the leaking coolant has been blown around by the fan.
Loose or broken fan belt	At the same time check that the fan belt is in position and the tension is correct. Adjust the tension if necessary. If it is broken and you have a replacement in the car, put it on. If not a temporary belt can be rigged up with a nylon stocking or one half of a pair of nylon tights. This will not last long but will probably enable you to get to a garage without too much overheating.
Leaking hoses	If it is apparent that one or more of the hoses are defective these will have to be replaced eventually but a short distance can be covered by wrapping the defective spot with tape and running with the radiator cap off to prevent the coolant being forced out of the leak under pressure. Do not top up the cooling system until it has cooled down for at least 30 minutes, or cold water going in may cause the metal in the block and head to contract too fast and crack.
Leaking radiator	Should it be established that the radiator has a leak this is a slightly more difficult problem if far from home. If a can of Radweld is kept in the car, top up the coolant to within about an inch of the top of the radiator (re-warm the engine to ensure the thermostat is open), pour in the Radweld refit the radiator cap and rev the engine a few times to let the Radweld circulate and be drawn into the leakage area and effect a seal. Any temporary measure used; the radiator should be removed and repaired by an expert as soon as it is practical.
Defective radiator cap	Remove the radiator cap and check that the seal is in good order and that the spring is not broken. The pressure cap blows off when a pre-determined pressure is reached (see specifications). Check that the correct cap is fitted.
Leaking thermostat housing gasket	If a leak is apparent from round the thermostat housing on the front of the cylinder head,

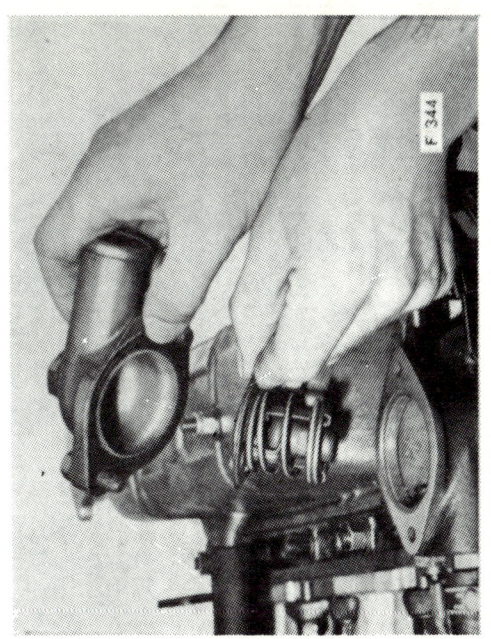

Removal of thermostat

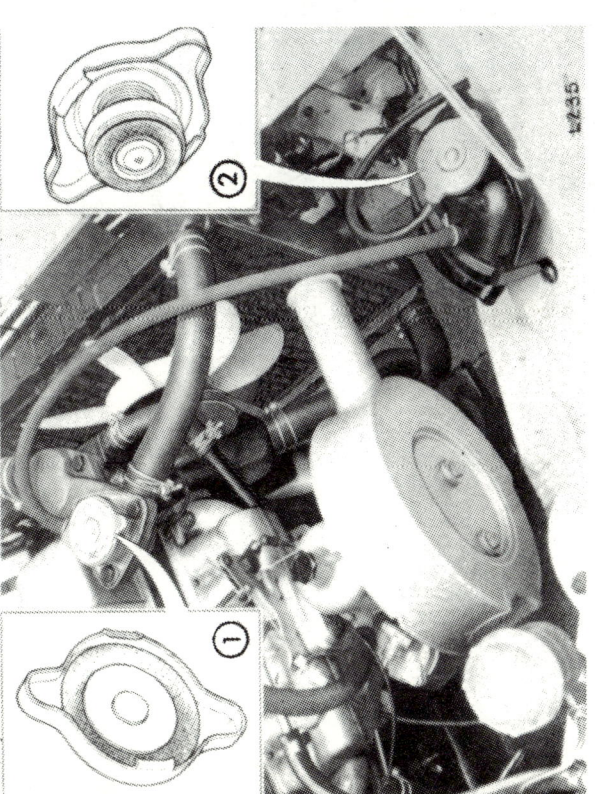

Cooling system

1　Radiator filler cup　　2　Pressure cap

General engine faults

the gasket must be renewed. To do this drain about 4 pints from the cooling system, loosen the upper hose at the thermostat elbow and pull it off the elbow. Undo the two bolts holding the housing in place and lift the housing and its paper gasket away. Examine the thermostat elbow to see if it is badly eaten away or corroded along its bottom edge. If it is, this has probably caused the leak and it must be renewed. Smear both the cylinder head and the thermostat housing mating surfaces with Hermatite or similar compound. Fit a new gasket and replace the housing, bolts and the upper radiator hose. Top up the cooling system, run the car and check for leaks.

Thermostat stuck in closed position

Remove the thermostat housing as described above and lift out the thermostat. If the engine is very hot and the thermostat is closed, remove it and at a later date replace it with a new one. Replace the housing and a new gasket as detailed above.

Blocked radiator either internally or externally

If the radiator fins are blocked with foreign matter this should be washed out with a pressure hose to allow the air to flow freely round the fins and do an effective cooling job. If a lot of oil is mixed in with foreign matter the best way to move this is to take the car to your local garage and have the radiator steam cleaned. With time the cooling system may lose its efficiency as the radiator becomes blocked with rust scales, hard water deposits and other sediment. To clean the system out, remove the radiator cap and the drain tap and leave a hose running in the filler hole for ten or fifteen minutes. At the same time probe the drain hole with a piece of wire to remove any built up deposits. In very bad cases the radiator should be reverse flushed. Place a hose over the drain tap and turn it on thereby forcing water up through the radiator and out of the top filler hole. This will loosen most of the dirt etc and the radiator should then be flushed out in the normal way.

Blown cylinder head gasket

This fault is recognisable by the fact that excess pressure is built up in the cooling system and water/steam is continually being forced past the pressure relief valve in the radiator cap and down the radiator overflow pipe. The car should not be driven any distance with this fault or major engine damage may result. Get it to your local garage and have a new gasket fitted. This fault may also be accompanied by oil appearing floating on the top of the water in the radiator.

Leaking water pump or water pump gasket

Check round the water pump for signs of leakage. If the leak is round the gasket this must be replaced, but if the water pump itself is leaking it is probably cheaper and easier in the long run to get a replacement unit rather than try to repair the faulty pump. To remove the pump, drain the cooling system and then remove the top and bottom radiator hoses. Also, if fitted, remove the heater pipe union from the rear of the pump. Loosen the dynamo/

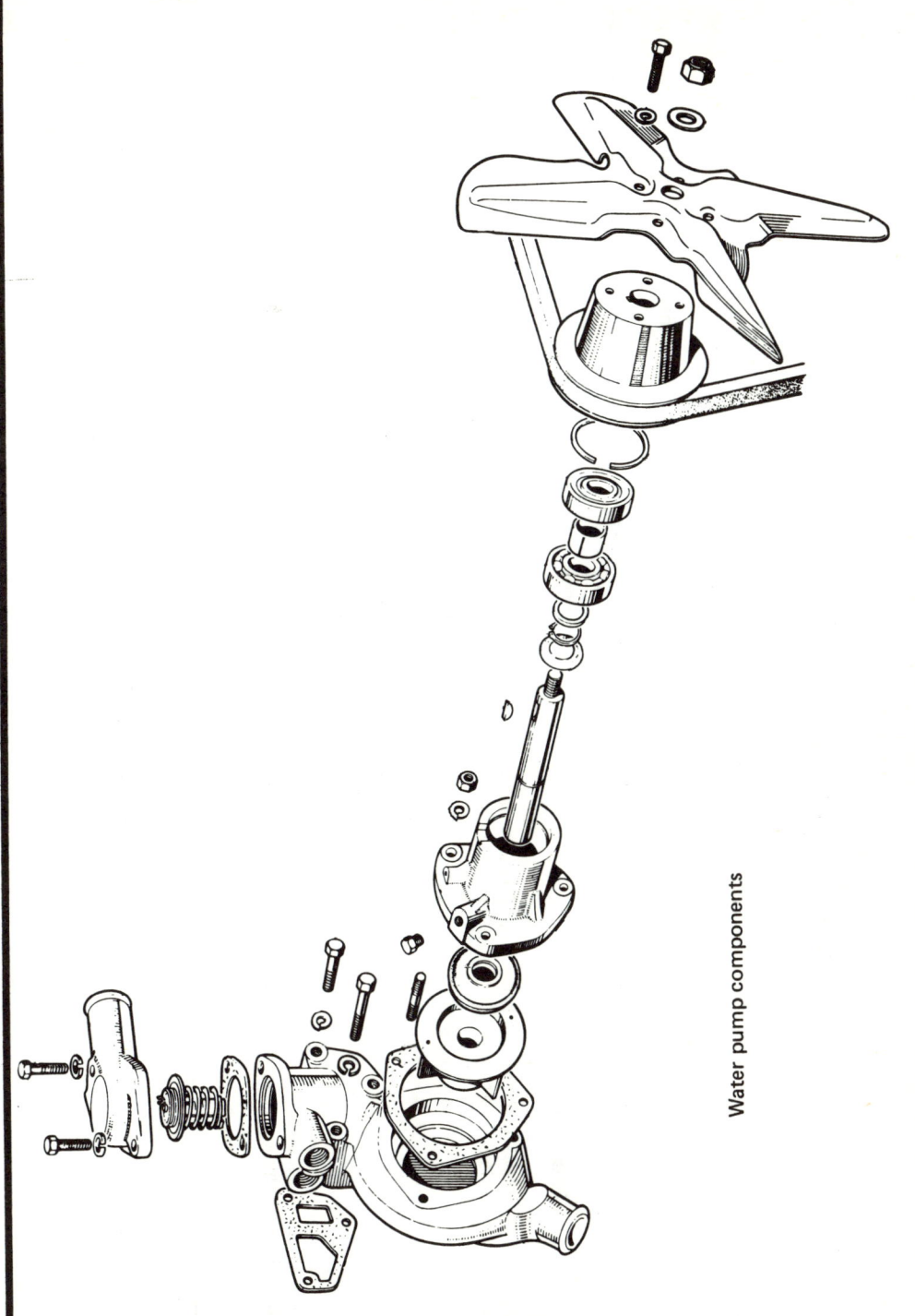

Water pump components

General engine faults

alternator securing bolts and swing the dynamo/alternator in towards the engine so the fan belt can be removed. Undo and remove the four bolts holding the fan and fan pulley to the water pump. Remove the fan blades and pulley and then undo the three bolts which hold the water pump to the cylinder block. Remove the water pump and its gasket. It is quite possible that a leaking gasket has been caused by a badly pitted or corroded water pump casing where it mates with the block. Examine this area carefully for signs of this fault. If the corrosion is very bad replace the pump as a matter of course. When replacing a pump and a new gasket smear the mating surfaces of the pump and block with Hermatite or a similar sealing compound to ensure a watertight joint. Replace the gasket, pump, fan pulley and blades. Reconnect the hoses, fill the cooling system and then run the engine and check that the leaks have been stopped.

Symptom Radiator continually requires topping up but no signs of external leakage

Possible Fault	Check and Remedy
Cracked cylinder block or head due probably to freezing coolant	Remove the dipstick and check to see if the oil level has risen or if there is any sign of water drops in the oil on the stick. If the level has risen then it is obvious that water has entered the sump and the oil is floating on the top of it. After the engine has been running for some time in this condition the oil on the dipstick may appear to be milky in colour. Oil will probably also have found its way into the cooling system and this can be seen by a film of oil floating on top of the coolant in the radiator. A leaking head or block may also be accompanied by the discharge of excessive amounts of steam from the exhaust pipe, even when the engine is thoroughly warmed up. If you suspect a cracked head or block consult your local garage immediately.

Symptom When engine is running ignition warning light fails to go out

Possible Fault	Check and Remedy
Loose or broken fan belt	Tighten or renew the fan belt as necessary.
Dynamo not functioning correctly	Check that the leads from the control box to the dynamo are firmly attached and that one has not come loose from its terminal. The lead from the D terminal on the dynamo should be connected to the D terminal on the control box, and similarly the F terminals on the dynamo and control box should also be connected together. Check that this is so and that the leads have not been incorrectly fitted. Make sure none of the electrical equipment (such as the lights or radio) is on and then pull the leads off the dynamo terminals marked D and

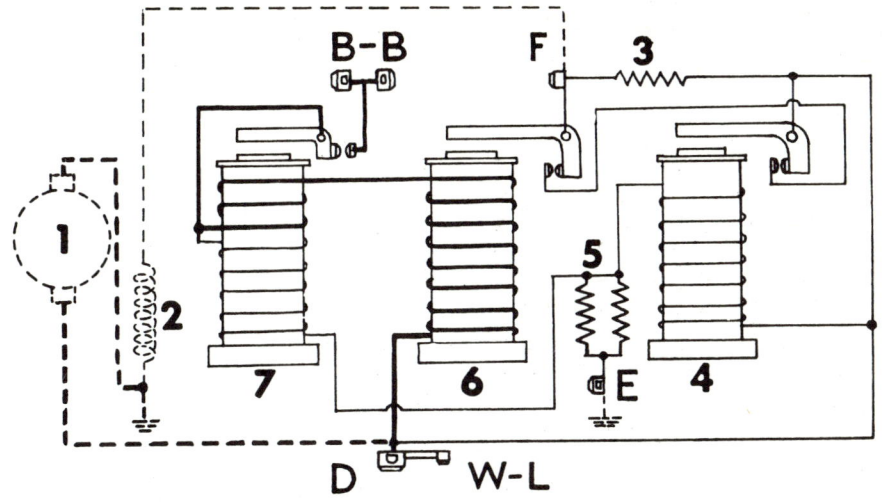

Electrical circuit for dynamo and control box

1 Generator armature 3 Field resistance   5 Swamp resistor   7 Cut-out relay
2 Field coils   4 Voltage ragulator   6 Current regulator

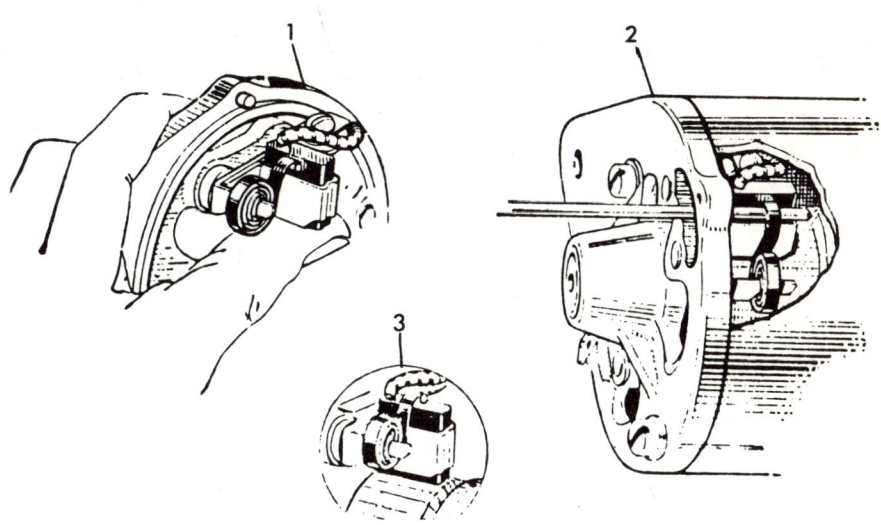

Fitting the commutator end bracket to 'Windowless' yoke dynamo

1 Trapping brush in   with spring   to brush   3 Normal working position
  raised position   2 Releasing brush on

General engine faults

F, join the terminals together with a short length of wire. Attach to the centre of this length of wire the positive clip of a 0–20 volts voltmeter and run the other clip to earth on the dynamo yoke. Start the engine and allow it to idle at approximately 750 rpm. At this speed the dynamo should give a reading of about 15 volts on the voltmeter. There is no point in raising the engine speed above a fast idle as the reading will then be inaccurate. If no reading is recorded then check the brushes and brush connections. If a very low reading of approximately 1 volt is observed then the field winding may be suspect. If a reading of between 4 to 6 volts is recorded it is likely that the armature winding is at fault. On early dynamos it was possible to remove the dynamo cover band and check the dynamo and brushes in position. With the Lucas C40–1 windowless yoke dynamo it must be removed and dismantled before the brushes and commutator can be attended to. If the voltmeter shows a good reading then, with the temporary link still in position, connect both leads from the control box to D and F on the dynamo (D to D and F to F). Release the lead from the D terminal at the control box end and clip one lead from the voltmeter to the end of the cable, and the other lead to a good earth. With the engine running at the same speed as previously, an identical voltage to that recorded at the dynamo should be noted on the voltmeter. If no voltage is recorded then there is a break in the wire. If the voltage is the same as recorded at the dynamo then check the F lead in similar fashion. If both readings are the same as at the dynamo then it will be necessary to test the control box.

Symptom	Possible Fault	Check and Remedy
	Control box not functioning correctly	The operation of the control box will have to be checked and this should be entrusted to your local garage or car electrical specialist.
	Alternator not functioning correctly	Take the car to the local Triumph garage or auto electricians.
Battery goes flat very quickly yet ignition warning light goes out normally	Battery defective	Check the specific gravity of the electrolyte in the battery. If one cell appears to be lower than the others then the battery may be defective and not holding its charge.
	Fan belt loose and slipping	Tighten the fan belt.
	Dynamo out-put not enough to charge battery	Check dynamo output as detailed above, if output low have the dynamo checked over by an expert in conjunction with the control box.
	Control box not operating correctly	Have an expert check the operation of the control box in conjunction with the dynamo.
	Alternator not charging	Take the car to the local Triumph garage or auto electricians.

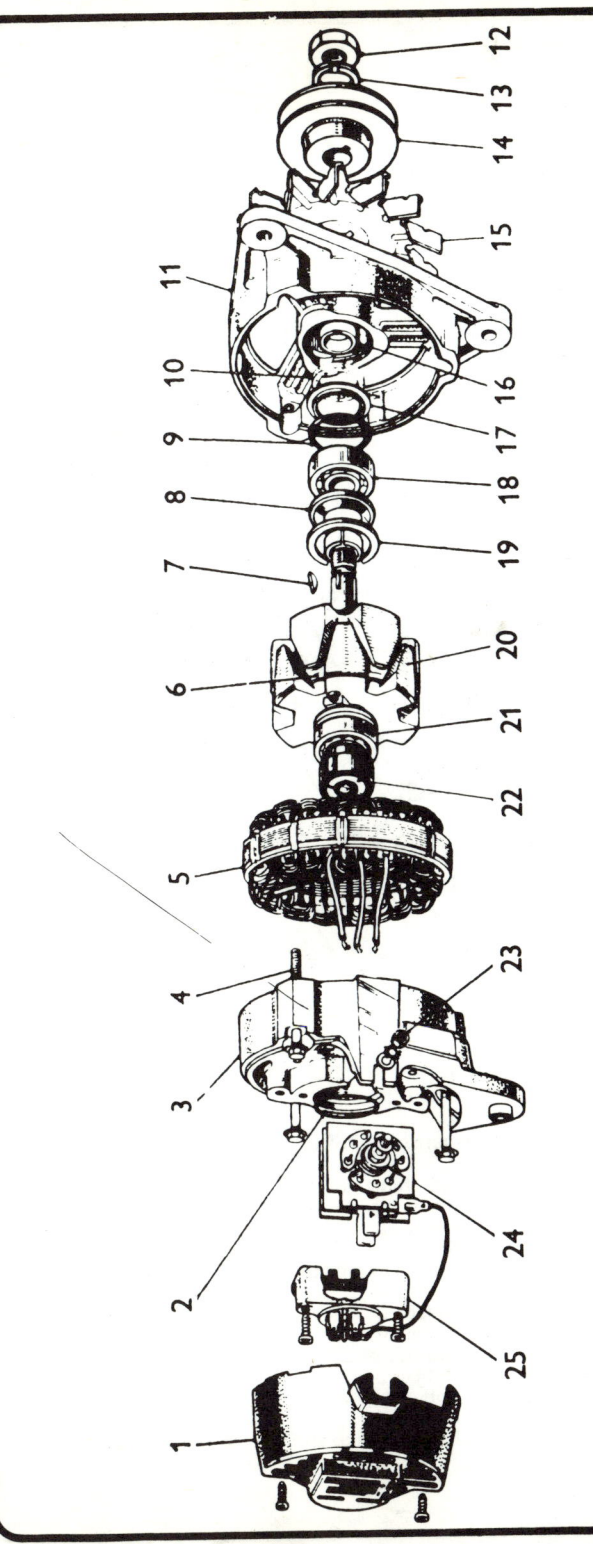

Alternator component parts

1 Moulded cover
2 Rubber 'O' ring
3 Slip ring end bracket
4 Through bolt

5 Stator windings
6 Field winding
7 Key
8 Bearing retaining plate

9 Pressure ring
10 Felt ring
11 Drive end bracket
12 Nut
13 Spring washer

14 Pulley
15 Fan
16 Spacer
17 Pressure ring and felt ring retaining plate

18 Drive end bearing
19 Circlip
20 Rotor
21 Slip ring end bearing

22 Slip ring moulding
23 Nut
24 Rectifier
25 Brushbox assembly

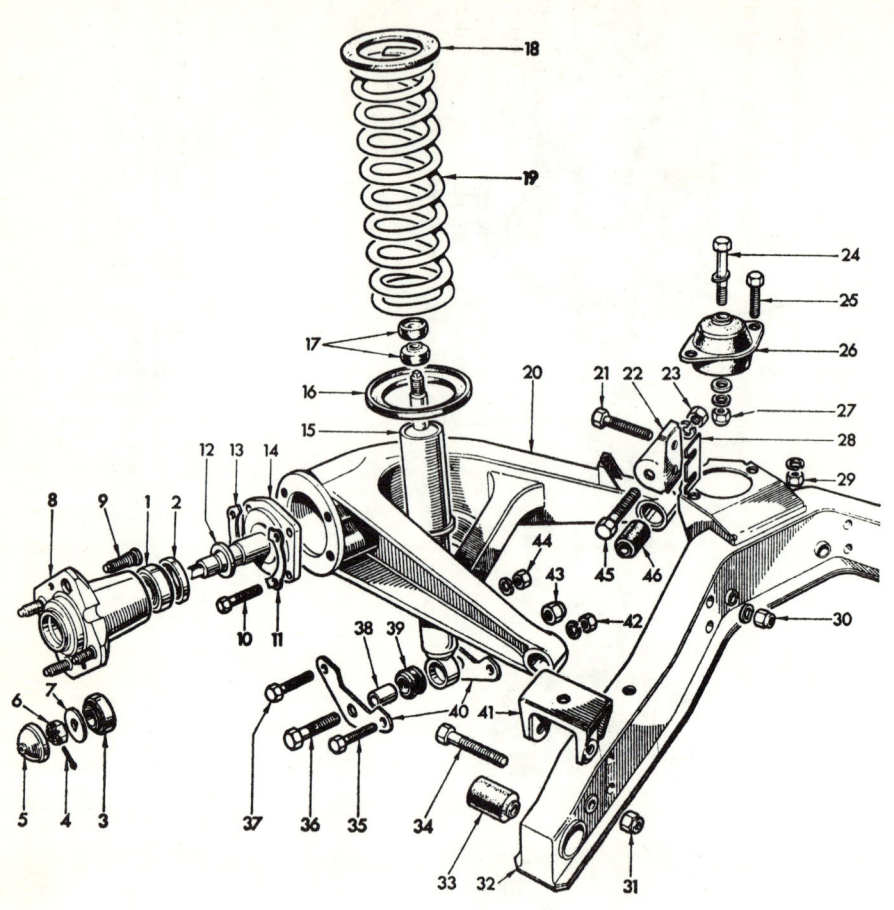

Component parts of rear suspension (1300)

1	Inner taper roller bearing
2	Oil seal
3	Outer taper roller bearing
4	Split pin
5	Grease cap
6	Slotted nut
7	Washer
8	Hub flange
9	Wheel stud
10	Bolt
11	Tab washer
12	Seal track
13	Tab washer
14	Stub axle
15	Damper
16	Rubber insulator
17	Rubber mounting
18	Rubber insulator
19	Road spring
20	Suspension arm
21	Bolt
22	Support bracket
23	Nut
24	Bolt
25	Bolt
26	Sub-frame rubber mounting, centre
27	Nyloc nut
28	Shim
29	Nut, mounting to frame
30	Nyloc nut
31	Nyloc nut
32	Sub-frame
33	Rubber bush
34	Bolt, sub-frame mounting
35	Bolt, plates to arm
36	Bolt, damper attachment
37	Bolt, plates to arm
38	Distance bush
39	Rubber bush
40	Mounting plate
41	Sub-frame mounting, outer
42	Plain nut
43	Nyloc nut
44	Plain nut
45	Bolt
46	Rubber bush

Other mechanical faults

Symptom Car tends to wander when driven in a straight line

Possible Fault	Check and Remedy
Tyre pressures incorrect or uneven	Check the tyre pressures at the first available opportunity and adjust them as necessary.
Wheels out of balance or out of alignment	Take your car to your local garage and have the wheels balanced and the wheel alignment checked on proper optical equipment.
Broken or weak spring	Have a good look round the springs to check for a broken coil. If a spring is badly weakened this will very often be noticeable by the fact that the car will appear to be lop-sided when standing on level ground.
Excessive wear in the steering linkage	To check if there is any excessive wear in the linkage, jack up the front of the car and examine all joints in the mechanism by pulling and pushing them. If there is excessive movement it is probable that replacement parts will be necessary and this job should be entrusted to your local garage. A lot of free play on the steering wheel when the car is at rest indicates considerable wear in the linkage, very often in the steering rack or flexible coupling.
Car incorrectly loaded	If you are carrying any reasonable weight of passengers or luggage make sure that the load is evenly distributed round the car and not all on one side as this can affect the handling and steering quite considerably.
Front wheel bearings worn or need adjustment	Check and adjust the front wheel conical bearings as described in the 24000 mile service schedule.

Symptom Steering becomes stiff after running normally

Possible Fault	Check and Remedy
Front tyre pressures too low	Inflate the tyres to the correct pressure as shown in the Specifications.
Lack of oil in rack due to leakage	Check the steering rack assembly for leaks particularly round the rubber bellows at either end. If these are torn they will require renewal.
Front wheels badly out of alignment	Get your local garage to check and adjust the front wheel alignment on proper optical equipment.

Other mechanical faults

Symptom Clutch slips

Possible Fault	Check and Remedy
Clutch adjustment incorrect	Take the car to the local Triumph garage and have clutch adjusted.
Oil or grease on the clutch linings or clutch worn out	If after checking the adjustment as above the clutch continues to slip the chances are that the friction plate will have to be removed. This will mean the removal of the clutch and should be entrusted to your local garage.

Symptom One or some lights do not come on when switch is operated

Possible Fault	Check and Remedy
Defective bulb(s) or fuses	Check fuses or replace the bulb in question. To make sure that it really is the bulb that is at fault check it in another location known to be functioning correctly.
Dirty or corroded connections at bulb holder	If the suspect bulb works in another holder then its own holder must be at fault. Thoroughly clean up the connector and bulb holder itself.

Symptom Pedal feels spongy when the brakes are applied

Possible Fault	Check and Remedy
Air present in the hydraulic system	Bleed the hydraulic system as described in the 24000 mile service schedule and check for leaks where air could have entered the system.

Symptom Pedal feels springy when brakes are applied

Possible Fault	Check and Remedy
After fitting new linings; this means that they are not properly bedded in	Allow a few days for the brakes to bed in by which time the springy feeling should have disappeared.
Loose master cylinder	Check the tightness of the bolts securing the brake master cylinder to the bulkhead.
Loose brake backplate or disc	Remove the brake drums or pads and check that the brake backplates or discs are secure. If found to be loose, tighten down the securing bolts.

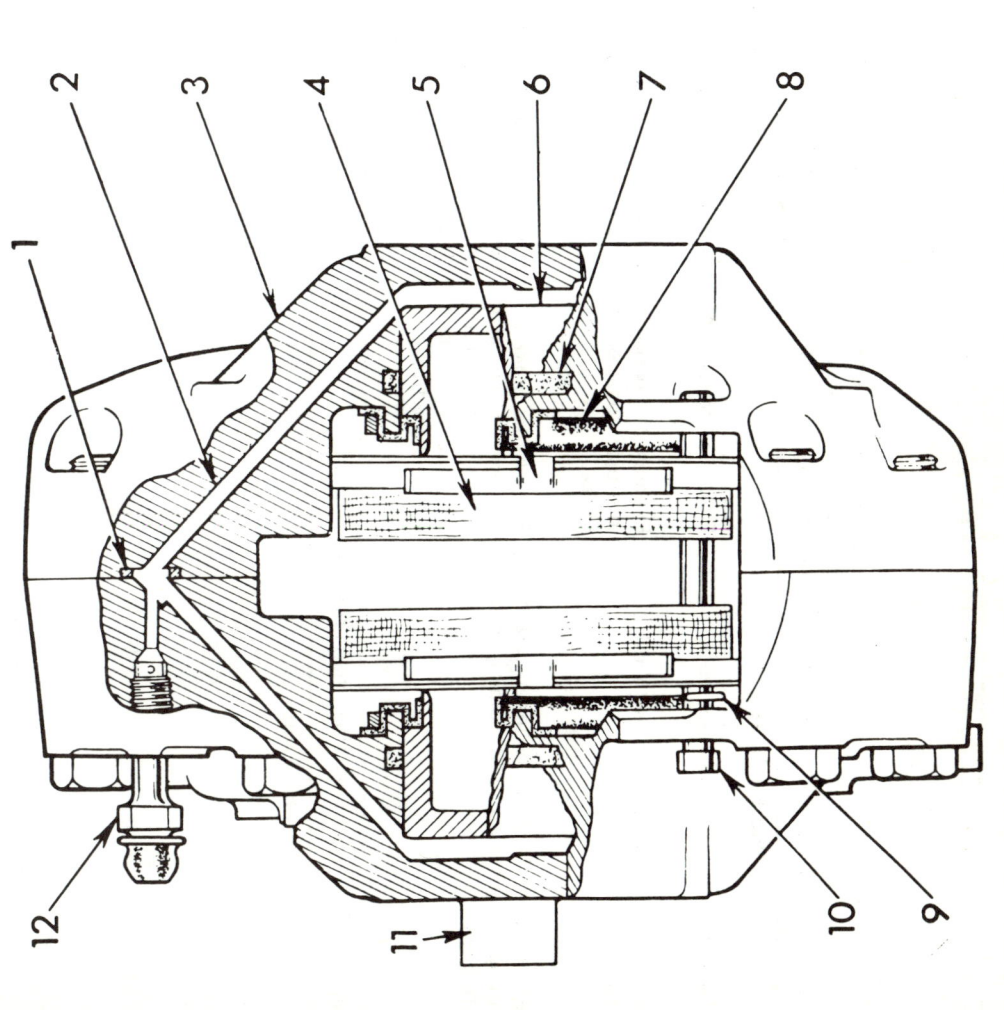

Front disc brake caliper assembly

1 Rubber 'O' ring
2 Fluid transfer chan-
nel
3 Caliper body
4 Brake pad
5 Anti-squeal plate
6 Piston
7 Piston sealing ring
8 Dust cover
9 Retaining clip
10 Retaining pin
11 Flexible hose connec-
tion
12 Bleed nipple

Other mechanical faults

Symptom Brake pedal travels a long way before the brakes operate

Possible Fault	Check and Remedy
Brakes need adjusting	Adjust the brakes as described in the 6000 mile service schedule.

Symptom Stopping ability poor even after adjustment and though pedal pressure is hard

Possible Fault	Check and Remedy
Brake linings or pads excessively worn	Examine and renew the brake shoes or pads as described in the 6000 mile service schedule.
Brake linings contaminated with oil or hydraulic fluid	Examine the brake linings and if found to be contaminated renew them. Also look for the source of contamination and eliminate it if possible, otherwise consult your local garage for advice.
One or more of the wheel cylinders seized resulting in the shoes not coming into contact with the drums	Remove the brake drums one at a time as detailed in the 6000 mile service schedule. Get an assistant to very gently press the brake pedal as each drum is removed and check that the cylinders are operating correctly. If a seized cylinder is located consult your local garage for a replacement to be fitted. On front disc brakes check that the pistons are free after having removed the friction pads.

Symptom Car pulls to one side when brakes are applied

Possible Fault	Check and Remedy
Brake linings on one side (opposite side from pull) are contaminated with oil or hydraulic fluid	Examine the linings and renew them as necessary as shown in the 6000 or 12000 mile service schedule as applicable.
Unequal wear on brake linings or pads	Adjust the brakes and if this has no effect on the pulling tendency remove the drums and examine for worn linings. Replace as necessary as shown in the 6000 or 12000 mile service schedule as applicable.
Wheel cylinder seized (on opposite side from pull) resulting in the shoes not coming into contact with the drum	Check the wheel cylinders as described above and have them replaced as necessary.

Other mechanical faults

Symptom Tyres are 'scuffed' on the edges and wear quickly

Possible Fault	Check and Remedy
Tyres under-inflated	Inflate the tyres to the correct pressure as shown in the Specifications.
Front wheels out of alignment	Have the wheels correctly aligned on proper equipment.
Front wheel bearings need adjustment	Adjust the front wheel bearings as described in the 24000 mile service schedule.

Symptom Tyre wearing quickly in centre of tread

Possible Fault	Check and Remedy
Tyres over-inflated	Reduce the tyre pressures to the correct level as in the Specifications.

NOTE: In the fault finding charts the owner is recommended to take his car to a local (preferably Triumph) garage to have many of the more complicated repairs attended to. If you have used this book successfully for Routine Maintenance tasks and wish to continue to carry out more complicated repairs yourself then you are recommended to use the Haynes Owner's Workshop Manual for the Triumph 1300/1500.

Castrol GRADES

Castrol Engine Oils

Castrol GTX

An ultra high performance SAE 20W/50 motor oil which exceeds the latest API MS requirements and manufacturers' specifications. Castrol GTX with liquid tungsten† generously protects engines at the extreme limits of performance, and combines both good cold starting with oil consumption control. Approved by leading car makers.

Castrol XL 20/50

Contains liquid tungsten†; well suited to the majority of conditions giving good oil consumption control in both new and old cars.

Castrolite (Multi-grade)

This is the lightest multi-grade oil of the Castrol motor oil family containing liquid tungsten†. It is best suited to ensure easy winter starting and for those car models whose manufacturers specify lighter weight oils.

Castrol Grand Prix

An SAE 50 engine oil for use where a heavy, full-bodied lubricant is required.

Castrol Two-Stroke-Four

A premium SAE 30 motor oil possessing good detergency characteristics and corrosion inhibitors, coupled with low ash forming tendency and excellent anti-scuff properties. It is suitable for all two-stroke motor-cycles, and for two-stroke and small four-stroke horticultural machines.

Castrol CR (Multi-grade)

A high quality engine oil of the SAE-20W/30 multi-grade type, suited to mixed fleet operations.

Castrol CRI 10, 20, 30

Primarily for diesel engines, a range of heavily fortified, fully detergent oils, covering the requirements of DEF 2101-D and Supplement 1 specifications.

Castrol CRB 20, 30

Primarily for diesel engines, heavily fortified, fully detergent oils, covering the requirements of MIL-L-2104B.

Castrol R 40

Primarily designed and developed for highly stressed racing engines. Castrol 'R' should not be mixed with any other oil nor with any grade of Castrol.
†Liquid Tungsten is an oil soluble long chain tertiary alkyl primary amine tungstate covered by British Patent No. 882,295.

Castrol Gear Oils

Castrol Hypoy (90 EP)

A light-bodied powerful extreme pressure gear oil for use in hypoid rear axles and in some gearboxes.

Castrol Gear Oils (continued)

Castrol Hypoy Light (80 EP)

A very light-bodied powerful extreme pressure gear oil for use in hypoid rear axles in cold climates and in some gearboxes.

Castrol Hypoy B (90 EP)

A light-bodied powerful extreme pressure gear oil that complies with the requirements of the MIL-L-2105B specification, for use in certain gearboxes and rear axles.

Castrol Hi-Press (140 EP)

A heavy-bodied extreme pressure gear oil for use in spiral bevel rear axles and some gearboxes.

Castrol ST (90)

A light-bodied gear oil with fortifying additives

Castrol D (140)

A heavy full-bodied gear oil with fortifying additives.

Castrol Thio-Hypoy FD (90 EP)

A light-bodied powerful extreme pressure gear oil. This is a special oil for running-in certain hypoid gears.

Automatic Transmission Fluids

Castrol TQF

(Automatic Transmission Fluid)

Approved for use in all Borg-Warner Automatic Transmission Units. Castrol TQF also meets Ford specification M2C 33F.

Castrol TQ Dexron®

(Automatic Transmission Fluid)

Complies with the requirements of Dexron® Automatic Transmission Fluids as laid down by General Motors Corporation.

Castrol Greases

Castrol LM

A multi-purpose high melting point lithium based grease approved for most automotive applications including chassis and wheel bearing lubrication.

Castrol MS3

A high melting point lithium based grease containing molybdenum disulphide.

Castrol BNS

A high melting point grease for use where recommended by certain manufacturers in front wheel bearings when disc brakes are fitted.

Castrol Greases (continued)

Castrol CL

A semi-fluid calcium based grease, which is both waterproof and adhesive, intended for chassis lubrication.

Castrol Medium

A medium consistency calcium based grease.

Castrol Heavy

A heavy consistency calcium based grease.

Castrol PH

A white grease for plunger housings and other moving parts on brake mechanisms. *It must NOT be allowed to come into contact with brake fluid when applied to the moving parts of hydraulic brakes.*

Castrol Graphited Grease

A graphited grease for the lubrication of transmission chains.

Castrol Under-Water Grease

A grease for the under-water gears of outboard motors.

Anti-Freeze

Castrol Anti-Freeze

Contains anti-corrosion additives with ethylene glycol. Recommended for the cooling systems of all petrol and diesel engines.

Speciality Products

Castrol Girling Damper Oil Thin

The oil for Girling piston type hydraulic dampers.

Castrol Shockol

A light viscosity oil for use in some piston type shock absorbers and in some hydraulic systems employing synthetic rubber seals. It must not be used in braking systems.

Castrol Penetrating Oil

A leaf spring lubricant possessing a high degree of penetration and providing protection against rust.

Castrol Solvent Flushing Oil

A light-bodied solvent oil, designed for flushing engines, rear axles, gearboxes and gearcasings.

Castrollo

An upper cylinder lubricant for use in the proportion of 1 fluid ounce to two gallons of fuel.

Everyman Oil

A light-bodied machine oil containing anti-corrosion additives for both general use and cycle lubrication.

Index

Other titles in the Haynes Owners Handbook/Maintenance Manuals Series

Ford Anglia 105E/123E	**75p**
Ford Capri 1300/1600	**75p**
Ford Corsair 1500	**75p**
Ford Cortina Mk 1	**75p**
Ford Cortina Mk 2	**75p**
Ford Cortina Mk 3	**75p**
Ford Escort	**75p**
Austin A35 and A40	**75p**
BLMC 1100/1300	**75p**
BLMC Mini	**75p**
Morris Marina	**75p**
Morris Minor 1000	**75p**
Hillman Avenger	**75p**
Hillman Imp	**75p**
Triumph Herald	**75p**
Triumph 1300/1500	**75p**
Vauxhall Viva HA	**75p**
Vauxhall Viva HB	**75p**
Vauxhall Viva HC	**75p**
Vauxhall Victor FB	**75p**
Vauxhall Victor FD	**75p**

More titles are in preparation

A full range of Owner's Workshop Manuals also is available from the publishers